The Persian Wedding Book

A Simple and Easy-To-Understand Guide
To Planning and Celebrating a Persian Wedding
(For Iranians and Non-Iranians alike)

BY

Christen Flack Behzadi, M. D.

Pascal Editions
New York

PASCAL EDITIONS
P. O. BOX 90889
ROCHESTER, NEW YORK 14609
United States of America

Book and Cover Design by Pascal Editions

First Edition, March 2013

The Persian Wedding Book
Behzadi, Christen Flack, M. D.
1st Ed., Rochester New York, March 2013

"Only from the heart can you touch the sky."

— *Jalal al-Din (Rumi)*

Dedication

*This book is sincerely dedicated to "Mamani"
and "Abu" -- Roya and Hedayat Behzadi.*

I have so much gratitude towards you both for welcoming me into your family with arms wide open. Thank you both a million times and again for teaching me to cook, and to cook Persian at that!

Most of all, dear Abu, thank you for sparking my interest in all things Persian. Your mid-week feasts, your dinner and dance parties, were truly a sight to be seen. The endless food, tea, sweets and good conversation into the wee hours of the morning opened my eyes to this beautiful culture and all it had to offer. Thank you for opening that door for me, thank you for your loving advice, thank you for all the sweet memories.

Dedication

*This book is also sincerely dedicated to my Mom, Jennifer, and my Dad,
John*

*Of all the things that parents sacrifice and do to help their children realize
their full potential, the two of you have done them all.*

*I'm grateful for everything you both have given me over all these years to
propel me towards all my dreams.*

*I especially thank you for giving me my dream wedding. If it wasn't for that
none of this would be possible.*

**Love,
Christen**

TABLE OF CONTENTS

FOREWORD

INTRODUCTION

PART I

Persian Immersion Camp
& The History of the Persian Wedding

PART II

The Courtship/Engagement Parties & Events

PART III

The Pre-Wedding Parties & Preparations

PART IV

The Persian Wedding

PART V

The Post-Wedding Celebrations

ABOUT THE AUTHOR

ACKNOWLEDGEMENTS

REFERENCES

PART I

Persian Immersion Camp
& The History of the Persian Wedding

Chapter 1: Let's Start with the Basics: *The meaning of "Persian," plus several other useful "must-know" terms, such as Aroos, Shahdamad and Sofreh Aghd*............................*pg* **28**

Chapter 2: Zoroastrianism: *Zoroastrianism and the historical roots of the Persian wedding*...*pg* **35**

Chapter 3: Persians & Their Parties: *Learn why Iranians have 15 million parties before the wedding. (Yes, partly it's because they like to party but there are other reasons too)*..........*pg* **44**

Chapter 4: The Groom: *Learn what to do, what your responsibilities are, and how to handle yourself, if you're the male lead in this very romantic affair*..*pg* **48**

Chapter 5: The Bride: *Learn what to do, what your responsibilities are, and how to handle yourself if you're the female star of the show. (Hint: The lady is on a pedestal and in the parlor, and* her *best manners are on display too)*.......... *pg* **55**

Chapter 6: Persian Hospitality 101: *This chapter will guide you through the customary manners of Persians for these events, and elsewhere, from three-hour good-byes and gifts to the playful game of Tarof Kardan to saying thank you six different ways*...*pg* **60**

Chapter 7: Persian Dance, Party Stamina, and Party Attire: *How to fake it until you make it in grand style*............*pg* **70**

PART II

The Courtship/Engagement Parties & Events

Chapter 8: The Persian Mother & Courtship Basics: *The Persian mother, the different kinds of Persian marriages and family meetings & greetings. Hint: even casual dinners have purpose in the getting to know you phase*.....................................*pg 81*

Chapter 9: Courtship Etiquette: *Attire, Guests, Gifts and Manners*...*pg 91*

Chapter 10: The Meeting of the Couple (Didar): *And the courtship of the couple (Ashnaei)*.................................*pg 94*

Chapter 11: The Suitor: *And the meeting of the families (Khaste gari)*..*pg 96*

Chapter 12: The Groom's Formal Proposal (Baleh-boran): *With notes on Shirini Khoran (The Eating of Sweets)*.............*pg 104*

Chapter 13: Namzadi (The Engagement): *The family extends an invitation to the entire community to celebrate the couple's engagement at a wildly fun and lavish engagement party called Namzadi*...*pg 121*

PART III
The Pre-Wedding Parties & Preparations

Chapter 14: Pre-Wedding Shopping: *On the agenda: a Holy Book, a mirror, two candelabra, and the bride's shoes and wedding gown – all gifts from the groom to his bride..........pg **128***

Chapter 15: The Wedding Table (The Sofreh Aghd): *A "how-to" guide on preparing the table, notes on the pros and cons of hiring a Sofreh Aghd designer, a page-by-page description, the symbolism, meaning and pictures of each item, plus plenty of advice to get you going in the right direction................pg **133***

Chapter 16: The Perfect Vendors for Your Persian Wedding: *How to find and hire the best team..................................pg **220***

Chapter 17: The Bridal Shower (Jahaz-Boran): *The bride's family prepares the couple's home furnishings (Jaheeziyeh), and then they present their items to the couple at the Jahaz-Boran..pg **230***

Chapter 18: The Threading of the Bride (Band-Andazan): *A few days before the wedding the bride begins her beautification for the big day. This is a special women-only party held for the bride, called Band-Andazan..................................... .pg **242***

Chapter 19: The Good Luck Party (Hana Bandan): *Finally, with the traditional goal of increasing the couple's luck, a large joyous party called Hana-bandan is held the night before the wedding...pg **246***

PART IV
The Persian Wedding

Chapter 20: The Legal Wedding: *On a specially designated day, a legal wedding is conducted for the couple*......................pg **261**

Chapter 21: The Start of the Day: *On a different day from the legal wedding, the Persian cultural wedding begins. A bride gets ready at the salon before the ceremony, and then is picked up by her groom*......................pg **270**

Chapter 22: The Burning of the Espand: *Before the ceremony, the espand is burned for the couple– a ritual intended to protect the bride and groom from "evil eyes"*......................pg **272**

Chapter 23: The Persian Wedding Ceremony (Aghd): *The formal Persian wedding ceremony takes place*......................pg **274**

Chapter 24: The Dove Release: *After the ceremony, a butterfly or dove is released*......................pg **308**

Chapter 25: The Grand Reception (The Jashn-Aroosi): *The Jashn-Aroosi is a wild, long, exciting, incredibly fun party where you eat yourself silly and dance until it hurts all night long. If you've had a very successful reception, you'll serve breakfast when it's over!*......................pg **310**

PART V
The Post-Wedding Celebrations

Chapter 26: Madar Zan Salaam and Patakhti: *Just because the wedding's taken place doesn't mean it's all over. After the wedding comes, there's the Madar Zan Salaam – the groom goes to thank the mother of the bride for raising such a wonderful daughter. Then a small party called Patakhti is thrown in the evening a few days after the wedding, just for the couple and their family, in order to celebrate and remember the happy wedding..pg 329*

Chapter 27: PaGosha, the Never Ending Ending: *Finally, the couple's families host a series of dinner parties one to welcome the new couple into the family and community as a whole. These on-going dinner parties are called PaGosha........pg 336*

Foreword

My life was proceeding along as planned in 2005. I had just graduated from The University of Michigan. I was accepted into medical school and was moving from Ann Arbor to Oklahoma City to start my first year and begin my lifelong dream of becoming a doctor. I was focused and motivated far more than any twenty-two year old probably should be. I had it all figured out and my life was moving in the direction I had planned. Then, the day before medical school started, I went to a pre-orientation party and met one of my classmates. His name was Pedram Behzadi. Once I met him, my life transformed in a magical way. My rigid plans delightfully began to disappear. We became the best of friends. We fell in love. Then, we became engaged to be married.

I was beside myself with happiness at the thought of living out my days with Pedram. I didn't care about anything else. I was fulfilled and happy. Most of everything else didn't matter in the way it had before. We could have been married in my back-

yard with two guests and that would have been enough for me. I quietly began planning for a traditional American wedding.

I bought many wedding magazines and was on my way. Until one day I had this idea. Out of no where, I all of a sudden wanted a Persian Wedding. That familiar intensity I was used to when I had a goal seemed to re-ignite within me. The determination I would soon realize would be much needed.

I wanted to have an authentic Persian wedding. To this day, I don't know why. But I knew we had to have a full-on, traditional, 100% authentic Persian wedding and nothing else would do. All I seemed to care about was making this magical otherworldly event be the perfect seal on the love we shared – even though I did not have the slightest clue how Iranians celebrated weddings. I had never been to a Persian wedding; I could find no how-to books on the subject. I had never seen one on TV. I had never even seen one on the internet. (When I began planning in 2008, the total number of Persian weddings on YouTube was zero!)

On top of that, I was planning to throw my gorgeous classic Persian wedding in the misty, faraway romantic realm of – Tulsa, Oklahoma. There are no Iranian caterers in Tulsa, Oklahoma. Few vendors had ever heard of a Persian wedding. Even fewer had ever worked on one.

It didn't matter. I was determined. What I didn't know I would learn. With my family's blessing and my Iranian mother-in-law enthusiastically on board, I went for it.

My Iranian mother in-law was a great help and a great support. But I couldn't call on her for everything. Being Iranian doesn't make you a Persian wedding specialist by profession; any more than being American allows you to automatically direct American marriage ceremonies. Moreover, she had one single focus: the wedding table (known in Farsi as the Sofreh Aghd). She needed to concentrate all her energy on making it perfect. Now and then close friends would come to the house at night, and she would carefully spread out items intended for placement on the table. There were many items! I learned a few Farsi words then, such as khalee, meaning "empty." "No empty areas!" one friend exclaimed in Farsi. So my mother-in-law went shopping, again, because she needed more decorations, more flowers, more of this, that and everything! No empty areas on the wedding table. Ever.

My job? My job was to do everything else!

Since my American family was completely in the dark about Persian weddings, they were not much help at that point. My parents did send checks from West Bloomfield, Michigan, and that most definitely helped. In Persian weddings, the groom and his family are supposed to pay for everything. My husband-to-be failed to mention this as I went out and charged up a storm. Fortunately he is now indebted to me for life, and so, after the nuptials, I've added those expenses to the dowry that he owes me. Every time we go shopping I don't hesitate to browse diamonds, brand names like Jimmy Choos and whatever else my heart desires. I may not be Persian, but I can shop like a Persian for sure.

But this shows how clueless I was. My family weren't the only ones in the dark. I was too, which meant I couldn't be very much help to me either. Could my vendors help? Forget it – that would be the blind leading the blind. My mother-in-law was so totally focused on setting the wedding table properly – a huge element in Persian wedding ceremonies – that there was little time for other advice. The wedding table had to be perfect! (Good news for you: follow the text guidelines and pictures in chapter 15, the "how to guide" for the Sofreh Aghd and you can be perfect right out of the box.)

Moreover, I was sworn to secrecy by her not to discuss our plans with the other Iranians in the community, and some of the secrets were kept secret even from me.

Why? Don't be ridiculous. Our Persian wedding had to be the best Persian wedding of all time! It wasn't *merely* going to be better than all the other Persian weddings held in Tulsa (which is to say, one in the five years previous and none in the three years following). It didn't matter whether we had stiff competition or not. We were going to have the best Persian wedding ever. Period!

So this is where my quest began. With no books to examine, no Persian wedding magazines to browse, no professional consultants to consult, no vendors to lean on, no other such weddings in the area to attend, I set out on a journey to know the Persian wedding.

Learning about how to do a Persian wedding meant doing research and studying even before I could begin to plan.

I sought out sources. I took notes. (I was in medical school at the time and all I ever did was take notes; I lived and breathed notes. If someone mentioned last night's football game, I would take notes.)

But research proved disheartening. There was not much in English about the Persian wedding — to put it mildly! I did find one book, Bijan Moridani's wonderful The Persian Wedding[1], which celebrated the incredible poetry of a fantastic ceremony with great beauty; it was so delightful to read.

I was in desperate need of advice and a planner. I needed a planner that didn't need to be flown in from Rodeo Drive in Beverly Hills, CA to Tulsa, Oklahoma, which has a lovely Rodeo but no Rodeo Drive. The internet, incredibly, was barren. Not even a good YouTube video (at least that part has changed, to my absolute delight).

I wanted a clear step-by-step guide in English on what to do, in what order, and I needed the meaning of it all explained. I am after all non-Iranian and I needed instruction in not only the wedding but in the

---

[1] I highly recommend that book. It is an historical study on the Persian Wedding and very well written. At one time his book was the only book available for English-speaking-only brides who "did not know what Persian means," and my copy of his book is still proudly displayed on my coffee table. I absolutely love reading it, and the artwork is delightful. All English-language readers who love or have ever been touched by the Persian wedding ceremony owe him many thanks.

customs as well. I needed to know if it was really a good idea to make the wedding table ourselves and what sort of music to play at the wedding. The book I was looking for didn't exist... Yet.

So – I gave up. After all, the English-language

book I wanted was just not there. I began searching for information, in Farsi. I ordered books in Farsi from Iran on this topic. And I kindly asked my mother-in-law to translate the books one by one for me into English. I read as much as I could. I did my best to teach my vendors what I was learning and to my amazement something magical happened. I noticed that the more I studied the Persian wedding, the more others came to share my interest and their expertise and help. These great people learned right along with me and became a huge support in creating something spectacular. My vendors listened and joined in the excitement. They eventually took over and with supreme creativity produced a spectacular wedding that I will always remember.

I took a lot of notes while I was doing my research. And after the wedding had taken place and my day as a bride began flowering into my life as a wife, I didn't put my notes away – I returned to them and began looking them over. An idea was tapping at the back of my mind. I realized something amazing. I had been searching and searching for a book in English that would tell me everything I needed to know about hosting a genuine, wonderful, spectacular Persian wedding. I couldn't find one anywhere. And now – here I was looking at it. I was holding in my hands exactly that book.

I had a vision but no real idea how my notes could become a coherent work, which could help other brides who were in my position, trying to plan a Persian wedding with no knowledge of Persian weddings. Given that I moved three weeks after my wedding from Tulsa, Oklahoma to New York for my residency, this seemed like a lovely but far-fetched idea at the time. Plus, these really were notes I used to

help me remember this term and that event's meaning. Essentially a pile of hand written scribbles, not carefully fashioned sentences inside bound covers – but, nonetheless I believed that all the material for a good book was there.

I just had to re-write it and turn my dashes and scribbles into readable English – English that would do justice to this beautiful and ancient ceremony.

I'm a physician by training, not a professional writer. So, it took time to put this together, three years to be exact. At that point, I gave a draft to my sister Courtney, who is a writer, and I had a very large drink while I prepared myself for her response.

She liked it!

The rest (after several more drafts) is history.

If at times this book seems like it has multiple story lines, it does. It is of course a story about the Persian wedding, as I understand it – from start to finish. It's a story about Persian culture and all the lovely ways this wedding celebration highlights the best, most charming and enjoyable aspects of Persian cultural ways.

It's a love story – mine. And of course, it's a step-by-step guide on how to plan, carry through and enjoy a Persian wedding of your very own.

This book's main goal, always, is to share all the things that non-Persians may not know about Persian

cultural ways, the events of the Persian wedding and the tone of the courtship/marriage process in Iranian culture.

I've had lots of fun writing this book. I hope that as you read it, you'll also feel the joy, love and enthusiasm for the Persian wedding.

My deepest wish for you is to have an even more beautiful, authentic and spectacular wedding of your very own. I wish for you to become totally inspired to create something more beautiful than I can even imagine. I look forward to seeing even more YouTube videos, magazines and books to come on this topic.

But above all, I wish you a lifetime of happiness, a marriage made of fairy tale dreams, and a life lived happily ever after.

Christen

Introduction

THE PERSIAN WEDDING OF YOUR DREAMS

No matter who you are, if you are looking to plan a traditional Persian Wedding, this book is here to help you. This book is your helpmate and your guide to arranging such an event. It contains all you need to know, whether you are:

• A person from any country who wants to better understand, honor and take part in an Iranian spouse's customs.

• An Iranian couple planning a full traditional wedding.

• An Iranian couple that wants to add some traditional elements to a more modern wedding.

• An Iranian spouse seeking to explain the ceremony to your non-Iranian spouse's relatives or to guests.

• A friend or family member who will be attending an Iranian wedding.

• Anyone who knows and loves Persian culture and wants to know more about one of its most beautiful and central ceremonies.

Perhaps you're an Iranian bride, newly engaged, eager to celebrate your Iranian heritage. Perhaps you're the mother of the bride, seeking to pass on the wedding customs and traditions of your beloved homeland, Iran, to your newly engaged son or daughter. Maybe you're an Iranian groom who wants to share the meaning and splendor of Iranian wedding customs with your non-Iranian bride. On the other hand, perhaps you're like I was – an American bride-to-be engaged to an Iranian, trying to plan a wedding that honors the customs and traditions of both cultures, without a clue about what a Persian wedding entails.

Once you're engaged, the clock starts running. You need to get everything done in an organized and timely manner. The photographer needs to be booked right away, as does the venue. The guest list must be made next and of course the most important decision must be made: how exactly do you want to celebrate the upcoming marriage? In this age of culturally blended couples, this is becoming an increasingly common and complex question. Marriage is a significant event in the life of the bride, groom and certainly their families too. The marriage traditions of each culture are beloved and sacred for all involved and honoring those traditions in some way even if

small and respectful certainly sets the loving, cooperative framework necessary for a strong and lasting marriage. Often with blended couples the marriage celebrations also become blended.

So, how do you "mix" for example an American wedding and an Iranian one? The simplest answer is that you take the best elements from both, the ones that you most want and love and put them there. True, it's much easier to add American elements because there are dozens of magazines, hundreds of books, thousands of wedding planners and caterers and wedding photographers and endless websites which cover every creative angle of an American wedding celebration from start to finish.

The Iranian Wedding on the other hand, has precious few guides available in English. Even in my research, I relied on both my own experiences and on imported books in Farsi from Iran which my mother in law carefully translated for me one by one (thank you for that, *Maman* Jan). I've brought all of my research together to create a source which can begin to make it easier to add those Iranian elements too.

So, the obvious question now is why. Why did I, an American bride new to Iranian culture, decide to go through all this – and even, eventually, to write a book about it? The short answer is that Persian culture simply fascinated me. The experience of my own Persian wedding alone was amazing, but I found I was getting a crash course not so much in wedding events as in the Iranian cultural tradition through the vehicle of an elaborate wedding celebration.

Of course much of this book is about how to plan and host an actual, elaborate Persian wedding celebration outside of Iran, which matters a great deal when it comes to preserving the bride's sanity. But it was learning about the culture that eventually caught my interest the most. I learned about the lengths hosts will go to simply honor a guest in their home; I learned how women are honored in these celebrations and how brides are courted at great length by the family of the groom; I learned about the amazing extent of Iranian generosity as I was given exorbitant amounts of gold bangles, diamonds, precious jewels and multiple hand-knotted Persian carpets. Everyone in my husband-to-be's family living in Iran sent me gifts of jewelry or carpets for the wedding. And when we went to visit Iran, I received even *more* gifts!

I love wearing and displaying those gifts – but it was the honor and love given to me continuously that so impressed me throughout our marriage celebrations. It was a peek into "the Iranian way." Learning those ways fascinated me from start to finish. Everything that seemed so simple was actually elaborate and meaningful and deeply symbolic.

And *fun!* Everyone was always having *fun.* I

had entered a world where joy was over-flowing, and time and again I saw that joyful energy overcome not only myself as we prepared for the wedding but also hundreds of our wedding guests, most of whom had never seen or experienced this magnificent event and all of whom were completely overtaken in the happiness and excitement.

We all know what it feels like to feel happy and carefree, to giggle in amusement or to dance ourselves silly. The gifts were delightful, but these gifts of the heart were even more delightful.

That said, I want you, the reader, to have a practical, informative guide as well. Once you see and experience the ceremony, once you begin to understand and take part in the culture, the joy and fascination will take care of themselves. But as lovely as Iranian culture is, planning this wedding when you have no idea what the Persian wedding even entails can be daunting. I was fortunate. I had questions at every turn, but I also had an Iranian mother-in-law who, despite being 36 years removed from Iran and in a community that did not celebrate many traditional Persian weddings, still somehow knew what to do. When she didn't, she would pick up her cell and either call her friends who called their friends in Iran, or she called her own family and friends in Iran. The process was like a metaphor for the marriage ceremony itself:

modern American technology used to help find and make sure all the ancient Persian traditions were preserved and passed on to me, an American bride.

A FEW POINTS OF CLARIFICATION

I would like to clarify something to all my readers from the beginning. I don't consider myself to be a formal historian of the Persian wedding ceremony. I did study what scholarly literature I could, but many of the things I learned while planning my wedding were told to me by Iranian friends and the Iranian family of my husband. I believed them to be fact because they told me it's the way things are done and always have been. Who would know better?

But I know that's a matter of debate. Some may say that a living tradition will always be more vital than dry scholarship, but still, accuracy and truth matter. Unfortunately, neither scholarly certainty nor popular certainty is always certain. There were some ceremonial details that I could not fully validate by any source no matter how hard I tried, and some were objects of controversy among the scholars themselves. Iranian culture is a culture of passionate love and nowhere more so than in the Iranian love of history, so let me politely ask for a little forbearance from academic Iranian readers or those mothers, grandmothers and great-grandmothers who surely

know these traditions much better than I.

Though I'm only a student in this area, not a scholar, I can truthfully claim that I have been a careful and reverent student, and that I come in peace to share something I find to be an incredibly beautiful part of the amazing culture that is Iran's. I can't say for sure that everything here is perfectly accurate because traditions evolve over time and because local traditions differ as well. I can say for certain that I adore Persian culture and Persian history and that I tried as hard as I could to be as accurate as possible.

So while I hope that you will find a good deal of interesting history from this book, remember that it is not a history book but a practical manual. I want to help couples in love today throw an incredible Persian wedding and to really feel Persian culture wherever they are in a way they'll remember for the rest of their lives. I want the parents and brothers and sisters of a non-Persian bride or groom not to be merely puzzled spectators at this fabulous event, but to dance wildly, clap joyously and eat themselves silly.

I should also clarify from the beginning that every event I will discuss from start to finish is *cultural*. These events were enhanced upon, re-thought and sewn into the fabric of mainstream Iranian culture during the times of the Persians[1]. Meaning these are cultural celebrations which are *100% non-denominational*. This was a strange concept for me initially to understand that there were so many purely cultural celebrations that Iranians of all faiths enjoyed which were not religious. As I would quickly learn, the Iranians are rich in history and culture and have held steadfast to that culture for centuries. These wedding traditions we know today were born from the times of the great Persian Empires which not only had vast empires but vast influence.

As influential as the Persians were centuries ago, they were also incredibly tolerant and famous for their welcoming attitudes towards locals in territories which they ruled. The Persians welcomed the

---

[1] *Please flip to chapter 1 of Part I, "Persian Immersion Camp," for a detailed description of the word 'Persian,' its meaning and distinction from the general term 'Iranian.'*

CHRISTEN FLACK BEHZADI, M. D.

beliefs and customs of the locals and in many cases began celebrating those customs as well; which is precisely how these wedding customs were born. (You'll learn more about this in Part I "Persian Immersion Camp.")

This is not to say that religious beliefs should be excluded, as they rarely are, just to note that how you choose to incorporate the religious aspect is up to you. In fact, Crescents, Crosses, Stars of David and other religious traditions are welcomed and their incorporation is encouraged at each step along the way. These are after all marriage celebrations which each religion honors in its own special way.

These celebrations of the Persian Wedding leave plenty of room for your own religious beliefs to enhance and personalize your experience, even if multiple faiths are to be celebrated and honored, there is room for that too. Always remember that two faiths can work together to create a beautiful, even ecstatic wedding ceremony. You see, where love is, God is, and where friends and family and bride and groom all come together to celebrate that love, God then is celebrated too.

Each couple will create their own celebration and certainly may have a slightly different twist on some of these events, so my goal is to give you the framework in this book and let you add the dazzle.

Now, with all that said, please come as you are and join in this celebration as Iranians of all faiths have for centuries.

There is room for everyone in these ceremonies, even an American bride like I was who "had no idea what Persian means."

So please consider me your friend in this process and prepare yourself for a very good time. Let's spread this joyful loving energy all around.

Most importantly, let's go have some fun getting married!

With love, from one ecstatic bride to you, the next to love the Persian wedding!

Christen

Part One:

Persian Immersion Camp

and

The History of the Persian Wedding

Chapter 1:
Let's Start With the Basics

BASIC WEDDING VOCABULARY
& THE MEANING OF PERSIAN

Aghd - Wedding

Aroos - Bride

Shahdamad - Groom

Aroosi (Arusi) - The Reception

Sofreh Aghd - The Wedding Table or Wedding Spread

Persian or Iranian?

Here I'd like to explain the meaning and use of the word "Persian" and how and why it differs from the word "Iranian." But I should immediately add that this is a subject of considerable and lively debate among scholars, historians and Iranians themselves. The debate mostly centers on how people want to be addressed. Some people don't mind Iranian, others prefer Persian.

Iran is a country with a very long, very ancient history of civilization dating back at least seven to ten thousand years. The ancient Iranian civilization led the way in creating organized society as we know it and all the joys and benefits that come with it, such as art and poetry, as well as innovations ranging from the courier post to massive imperial administration.

The original people who formed the country we know as Iran were called, thousands of years ago, Aryans. The name Iran in fact derives from the term Aryan, and means something like "Land of the Aryans." To be Iranian means to be, however distantly, from Aryan descent.

The Aryans were not initially a united, homogenous group of people. Like many large ancient peoples, they were divided into tribes. These tribes had their own traditions and cultural tendencies. For example, the Medes tribe settled in the north of Iran. One of the largest Aryan tribes was the Kashi tribe which was settled in Kashan, Iran. An area in the north of Iran, near Lake Urima, became the location where one of the enduring world religions, Zoroastrianism, was born. The most famous Aryan tribe, the Persians, also known as the Parsa tribe, settled in the southern region of Fars in Iran. The Fars region of Iran is where current day Shiraz is located, as well as twenty-three other provinces, including the beautiful town of Kazerun.

It was the Aryan tribe of the Persians who lived in Fars who would go on to create the great dynasties and societies for which all of Iran became famous. The

Persians grew into a vast empire which came not only to eventually rule all the other Aryan tribes, but also to expand over much of the Middle East. In time, the Persian Dynasties made the growing religion of Zoroastrianism the official religion of the region, which to various degrees touched all the regions of the Middle East to this day.

The Persian dynasties ruled so much of what is currently known as the Middle East for so long that many historical writers at the time began referring to all of Iran simply as Persia, despite the fact that Persians were only one of the many tribes present in Iran. The term stuck, however, and it was not until the early 1900s that the rest of the world abandoned the term Persia and Persian to refer to the area and its people and began using the words Iranian and Iran.

This is where some of the confusion and heated debate begins. Many Iranians call themselves Persian whether they're of Persian tribal decent or not, and some people do not agree with this. Others do not agree with the term Iranian and believe Persian is more descriptive of the ancient cultural identification. There were many Aryan tribes, but the Persian tribe and the Persian dynasties established the organized cultural framework that permeated the life of all Iranians, whatever their tribal origins. Persian culture became the core culture with which all Iranians came to identify. If not for the Persian dynasties and their efforts to unite all the Aryan tribes into a cohesive cultural group, we might never have had the strong, united community that we know as the Iranian people today.

Some may find questions of tribal Persian heritage to be only a scholarly issue now – culturally; Iran has been Persian for millennia. But it continues to matter. The Persian Dynasties were the ones that first made the growing Zoroastrianism the official religion. Celebrations of Zoroastrian festivals such as Nowruz (the New Year celebration), Chahar shanbeh-suri (the jumping-of-the-fire celebration before the New Year) and Shab-e-yalda became the cornerstone of all Iranian cultural celebrations under the great Persian dynasties. And during this time, a uniquely Persian way of celebrating marriages was established.

So, while technically "Iranian" and "Persian" are distinct, nearly everyone, Iranian or not, uses the terms loosely and interchangeably, much like everyone says "America" or "United States." It's a difference that makes very little difference.

Given that the Persian dynasties united Aryan tribes into what eventually became a unified Iranian culture, it would be just as correct to call this book, "How to Plan an Iranian Wedding," as "How To Plan A Persian Wedding." After all, Iranians of all religious

faiths still identify culturally with these customs and ceremonies and have these same celebrations.

I use the word Persian because the traditions are so very traditional and so ancient that they seem to naturally deserve the term "Persian" which described them for so many thousands of years, as opposed to the Twentieth Century "Iranian," which is no less accurate but perhaps less evocative of the rich history that all Iranians honor. Plus while the great Persian dynasties certainly passed on their own tribal traditions, they also incorporated many other Iranian traditions into the one mainstream Persian culture that over long centuries solidified into the cultural fabric of all Iranian people.

The cultural cohesion uniting Iranians of all faiths has now flowered into a strong unity of cultural identification. This has benefited us non-Iranians too, by allowing us to share and enjoy the beauties of Iranian culture through the cultural events – supremely, the Persian wedding.

Chapter 2:

Zoroastrianism

SYMBOLS
AND THEIR MEANING AND ORIGIN
IN THE MODERN DAY
PERSIAN WEDDING CEREMONY

The Persian wedding is like a Persian tapestry: it can be enjoyed without a historical or scholarly understanding of the meaning of all the symbols and colors so beautifully evident throughout. But understanding can give that enjoyment an added depth.

The Persian wedding derives from Persian culture and in many respects that culture derives from Zoroastrianism, the ancient and unique religion of Iran. Below is a very brief discussion of Zoroastrianism and its influence on the Persian wedding ceremony. I've included it to give those unfamiliar with that faith and its history a way to better understand both the Persian wedding and Persian ways.

What follows is, of course, only an introduction and is in no way meant to be a complete historical study. This book is written out of pure love for those in love, and for all of us who have found ourselves planning a Persian wedding with little or no prior knowledge of the customs.

An Ancient Heritage

Persian history dates back almost seven to nine thousand years to the very beginnings of civilization. Its contributions to history – even to the history of romantic love – are long and distinguished. Excavations at Haiji Firuz Tepe in northwestern Iran credit ancient Persia with the discovery of wine in 5000 BC. The Tar, or lute, which led to the modern guitar, is also credited to the Persians at that time. Tulips were first cultivated in ancient Persia, and love letters might never have been written without the ancient Persian creation of the courier post.

Ancient Persia gave us Backgammon and Polo, and ice cream and the cookie – but also the first brick, from which all architecture would derive; the first banking system; mighty Empires that connected the peoples of the West with those of Central Asia and south-western Russia; and (not least) the Zoroastrian religion, at one time arguably the largest religion in the world and one whose tenets and symbols still underlie the tradition of the Persian wedding.

Zoroastrianism derives from the teaching of the prophet Zoroaster (also known as Zarathustra) in roughly the sixth century before the Christian era. In Zoroastrianism, there is a single creator, Ahura Mazda, who is entirely good, and who is locked in combat with evil (druj) which actively tries to destroy the creations of Mazda, just as Mazda actively sustains it. The religion dwindled when Alexander III of Macedon invaded the region, and it was further pushed from its central role by the triumph of Islam, which ended the Sassanid Empire in 651 C.E. and toppled Zoroastrianism from its role as the official religion.

But the political power of the Persian dynasties lent Zoroastrianism immense prestige in ancient times, and that prestige persists even in modern times. Zoroastrian attitudes, understandings and cultural modes are not a thing of the past. Their influence continues. The Persian wedding doesn't have to be a Zoroastrian wedding, though it can be. Nor is the ceremony itself a legal wedding anywhere outside Iran. Persian weddings are essentially secular, and couples must legally formalize their union later in a court of law.

But Zoroastrian elements permeate it everywhere, like bright threads in a rich Persian tapestry.

Zoroaster is said to be the first religious figure to originate the concepts of pure good and pure evil, and the first to originate the idea of free will, but his main influence on Iranian thinking may be his view that submission to the divine must not be merely passive but active and not only active but subjective: Zoroastrians advocate a continual striving for goodness not only in deed but in thought.

As a faith, it is perhaps best summed up by the following phrase from the Zoroastrian Heritage Institute:

> On these three noble ideals
> be ever intent:
> The good thought well thought
> The good word well spoken
> The good deed well done

This creed of "good thoughts, good words and good deeds" unites Zoroastrians around the world and is a guiding percept among Iranians. Hence it's not suprising that the modern day Persian wedding ceremony is overflowing with words and symbols expressing good wishes (good thoughts) for the bride and groom. Good thoughts are fostered all throughout the ceremony. From the espand (a spice which is burned over the heads of the bride and groom to eliminate bad energy from people not wishing the best for them) to the wedding spread in front of which the couple will sit to be married, the Zoroastrian call for an abundance of purity in thoughts, words and deeds is everywhere. Items all across the wedding spread are symbols and are symbolically placed to express good wishes for prosperity, for fertility and for a long, sweet and healthy marriage for the couple, their families and everyone attending.

The Zoroastrians use fire and water as part of most religious rituals. In Zoroastrianism, water (apo, aban) and fire (atar, adar) are agents of purity. Both water and fire are considered life-sustaining, and Zoroastrians typically pray in the presence of some form of fire. Fire sprang from water, in the Zoroastrian cosmogony, and so while fire is considered a medium through which spiritual insight and wisdom comes, water is considered the source of that medium and that wisdom. (Given these attitudes, it's hardly surprising that on the wedding spread at the ceremony there will be two large candelabras to symbolize fire or that many Persians prefer to have their ceremony held near a body of water for good luck.)

It certainly can't be said that the Persian wedding is only a diluted version of the Zoroastrian wedding. Iran is also home to a rich Sufi tradition. One of the

world's greatest mystical Sufi poets, Jalal ad-Din Muhammad Balkhī, known to the West as Rumi. His life-long literary advocacy of goodness, charity, limitless tolerance, positive reasoning and awareness through love was shared by many other mystic and Sufi poets of Persian literature and was rooted in the concept of tawhid – union with the Beloved. The Beloved might sometimes be a person, sometimes an experience like beauty or a concept like truth, but at its core it is identification with God. In each case, however, the poet's longing and desire to escape from separation and aloneness and to ecstatically unite with the Beloved was felt to be the great goal of all spirits – a celebration of love and union which the Persian wedding ceremony in so many ways beautifully reflects.

The Persian wedding is the coming-together of many influences over many, many centuries, but has its own unique and distinct flavor. Yet its uniqueness is accommodating. The wedding ceremony of the faithful religious Zoroastrian couple is different from the modern day Persian wedding ceremony and embodies many distinct practices and rituals. The modern Persian wedding can be a novel and non-denominational ceremony, one that over the centuries has come to include the attitudes and culture of non-Zoroastrian Iranians as well.

It might be said that in the modern Persian wedding, the explicitly religious Zoroastrian elements were gradually eroded by time, while the beauty and color was retained, all to better allow Persians of all faiths, intent on having the most joyous and meaningful event possible, a ready and resplendent framework to accommodate it. The final result is a ceremony which is as beautiful as ever, but more cultural than religious.

That said, the modern day Persian wedding is as vibrant and exciting as ever. It is the practice of many people outside Iran to hold a legal ceremony separately, but the traditional marriage remains central – the heart of the beginning of the union, a beautiful ceremony, wild and rich with symbolism and love.

As couples sit down at the Sofreh Aghd on their

wedding day, awareness of the meaning and symbolism behind every item on the spread and every part of the ceremony can only enhance the splendor of the moment and the depth of emotion underlying it.

As one of the more famous marriage poems of Rumi expresses it:

May these nuptials be blessed for us,
    may this marriage be blessed for us,

May it be ever like milk and sugar,
    this marriage like wine and halvah

May this marriage be blessed with leaves and fruits
    like the date tree;

May this marriage be laughing forever, today, tomorrow,
    like the maidens of paradise.

May this marriage be the sign of compassion
    and the approval of happiness
        here and hereafter;

May this marriage be fair of fame, fair of face
    and fair of omen as the moon in the azure sky.

I fall silent, for words cannot describe
    how the spirit has mingled with this marriage.

Chapter 3:
Persians and their Parties

When I began researching this chapter, I asked my father-in-law, "Why do Iranians love to party so much?"

"Because Iranians enjoy life," he said.

I suddenly understood. What he said and the way he said it were so simple and endearing that I needed to look no further to know why each step in an Iranian courtship and marriage seemed to have so many bells and whistles. Iranians enjoy life. It's that simple. They value the experience of living and have made it part of culture to enjoy it in the company of others as often as possible. Friendship isn't reserved for those who have passed enough tests to be allowed to invade your personal space. People are welcomed. Everyone is considered a friend till proved otherwise. Guests are welcome without notice needed, get the best seats, are served first and always honored. When two friends gather for dinner, it turns into a feast. And even for only two friends on a Tuesday evening, there will likely be music and dancing and laughter. The door is always open in an Iranian home for additional guests to join, and Persian meals are customarily prepared preemptively large for this purpose.

Having a celebration isn't something special. It is something you can't avoid! The idea of vivid celebration and fellowship is a part of every day; so special events like weddings pull out all the stops.

Iranians frequently invite friends to what others would call lavish if not spectacular dinner parties on a regular basis. To be Iranian is almost by definition to be polished and expert at hosting events. So, when there's a definite occasion for a large and lavish celebration such as a wedding, is it any wonder that the preparations and the ultimate celebrations become even more over the top and elaborate?

So, yes, Iranians do "love to party." But I've come to think that this love for parties springs

from a deeper love for togetherness.

I've learned that Iranians truly value closeness, not only their own children, spouses, parents and extended families, but also to their friends' children, parents and their extended families. You could almost say that the entire culture is one large extended family.

This deeper connection is what truly unites the community. Constant pleasant personal connection with others, combined with a culture that encourages simple direct appreciation for the joys of daily life such as a good meal, a hot tea, a walk in the park. Iranians are world-famous for their hospitality precisely because of this attitude.

Chapter 4:
The Groom

Responsibilities of the Groom and the Family of the Groom: The Traditional Division of Financial Responsibilities In the Persian Wedding

In a Persian wedding, the financial responsibilities of the bride and groom and their respective families are traditionally very clear and distinct. Some leeway may be allowed and negotiation may (and almost certainly will) take place, but only in already settled-upon areas. By and large, tradition dictates who pays for what.

This has its benefits. By making tradition the arbiter of who will provide each item needed for the couple, it not only minimizes possible friction, it

enables families to save and prepare for their contributions gradually over the course of a lifetime, which most people do.

Those who have great wealth will put their utmost into these celebrations.

Those who are rich in love and time will stop everything and devote nearly all their love and time to making these celebrations spectacular, creative, joyful and beautiful for the couple.

Parents will literally give anything and everything they have for the wedded couple.

And yet, these responsibilities are not a burden but a joy. Because in time the new family that emerges from the wedded couple will circulate their own love and their own time and assets and their growing wealth as well. What is received from family is passed on to family.

Financial Responsibilities of the Groom and His Family

The groom and his family traditionally provide:

1. Small gifts for the bride and her family during the initial meetings, such as the Khastegari or Baleh-boran, For instance, it's customary to bring sweets or a basket of flowers. Gifts need not be expensive: fruit, flowers or candies are all acceptable. But coming empty-handed is not customary – it may well be considered insulting.

2. The engagement band and the wedding ring for the bride.

3. The home (or, nowadays, arrange for an apartment or condominium) for the couple to live in when they are married. Purchasing a new home is considered the more traditional.

4. The bride's wedding gown and her wedding ceremony shoes.

5. Coverage for all costs related to the wedding ceremony and the reception.

6. A Mariyeh (a dowry) for the bride.

7. A Shirbaha ("The Price of The Milk") for the mother of the bride.

Historically speaking in Iranian culture when a girl is married, she is in theory leaving her family and joining the groom's family. So whereas before

the marriage the father of the bride was financially responsible for her, now her new family, the groom and the family of the groom, are financially responsible for her. So grooms and their families are expected to be completely prepared to ensure financial comfort, safety and stability for the bride even before the bride and groom are married. There should be sufficient assets in place for the bride well before the concluding ceremony. These assets are provided with love and are intended to ensure that if anything at all happens to the groom, she will have sufficient assets and to live in security and comfort.

The viewpoint from which these things are given should be understood clearly too. Some may imagine that a culture as highly traditional as the Iranian one may insist that brides be completely financially dependent on the husband or patriarch of the family. Nothing could be further from the truth. Brides are given assets and gifts during the Persian wedding ceremony precisely so that they can develop financial independence. Gifts given to the bride are hers and hers to keep. They are hers to use to maintain her own independent financial existence.

At the same time, it should be borne in mind that these assets are not viewed as assets that are taken away from the groom's family and spent on someone outside it; rather, they are assets that circulate within the family, since the marriage is bringing a new member into the family. Also, the assets bestowed on the bride are not necessarily, or even in most cases, classic financial assets such as stocks, bonds or hard currency. Later in the wedding chapter, for instance, you'll learn that brides are often given significant amounts of jewelry when they marry. Everyone – literally everyone, from both families – will bring her expensive jewelry. The jewelry isn't given purely for decoration (partly for decoration, yes). Jewelry is given to the bride for securing her own independent financial future.

Is jewelry mandatory? No, but Jewelry is often among the gifts. One of the purposes, historically, of "negotiation" meetings between families before the couples are engaged is to discuss these matters and agree to them. Gifts can be many in number and of many kinds: gold coins, precious objects, cars, planes, household appliances, holy scriptures, smart phones, iPads, real estate, show or vacation tickets or a kiss.

Always remember: the meaning of each gift is not the physical object itself. The objects are only surrogates for the real gifts – signs and symbols of the love, gratitude, honor and appreciation that are truly being given.

THE PRICE OF MILK (SHIRBAHA)

Shirbaha, literally means the price of milk in Farsi. It is a gift given to the mother of the bride intended to cover "the price of the milk" that the mother gave to her daughter. There is no customary Shirbaha. It can be monetary, symbolic small or large depending on the family's wishes. If a monetary gift is received, the mother of the bride typically uses the money to purchase items for the jaheeziyeh (home furnishings).

THE DOWRY (MARIYEH)

A dowry is a financial gift given to the bride before the couple is married. The dowry in Farsi is called a Mariyeh. The Mariyeh need not be a million-dollar deed to a home – although sometimes it is. It's quite common to have a symbolic Mariyeh, for example, a piece of rock candy and a holy book. It's also common to give extra jewelry to the bride.

The idea is to provide assets to the bride, which can be spiritual or even aesthetic, but is almost always, to whatever degree possible, financial as well. One aspect of the Mariyeh is to demonstrate to the bride, her family and the community the ability of the groom and his family to provide for the bride and keep and support her in financial comfort.

Chapter 5:
The Bride

RESPONSIBILITIES OF THE BRIDE AND HER FAMILY

The bride and her family are traditionally responsible for the following:

1. Hosting the Khastegari (Suitor comes to visit)

2. Hosting the Baleh-boran (Groom proposes)

3. Hosting the Namzadi (Engagement party)

4. Hosting the Hana-Bandan (Good Luck Party)

5. Providing furnishings for the couple's home (Jaheeziyeh)

6. Hosting a party celebrating the Jaheeziyeh (Jahaz-Boran)

7. Purchasing an engagement/wedding band for the groom

The first part of the Persian wedding process revolves around the bride and the groom and their families – especially their families – getting to know each other. So naturally, there are meetings. In the beginning, the responsibility for hosting those meetings falls on the bride's family. It goes without saying that the bride's family is expected to be gracious, warm, generous, welcoming and the perfect hosts in every way. While it's not untrue to say that that's how Iranian families like to see themselves as treating every guest, it is of course particularly true when they open their home to the potential future husband of the bride and when the guests may turn out to become family member themselves.

Although there is a great deal of pure socializing, neither side is there purely to socialize. The bride's family at this stage will host the traditional negotiation events – the Khastegari and the Baleh-boran. However, these events are far from pure negotiation.

A modern way of putting it would be to say that the bride's family would host a dinner in their home, in which both families as a whole come together (Khastegari) and later host a dinner where both families come together to witness and then celebrate the khastegar's (the suitor's) proposal (Baleh-boran). The bride's family also hosts an official engagement party (Namzadi) which the entire

extended family and community is invited to celebrate.

Another responsibility of the bride's family is to host something like a "spa day" (Band-Andazan) for the bride, her female friends and female family members, in which they both socialize and support the bride-to-be as she prepares her face (waxing and threading) for the wedding. A few days before the wedding, the bride's family also hosts a Good Luck party for the couple (Hana-bandan) to kick off the wedding events.

Meetings, get-togethers and contacts between family members aren't restricted only to these occasions – there's nothing forbidding the father of the groom from meeting the father of the bride in a restaurant for coffee, for instance, or from the bride and her groom's sister going shopping together. But the above named events are the milestones of the engagement process, and they are hosted – fully and elegantly – by the bride's family.

The other significant responsibility of the bride's family, initially, is financial. Specifically, they are expected to provide the furnishings for the new home of the couple (the Jaheeziyeh).

The Jaheeziyeh is fairly important. Some parents

with daughters will begin preparing for their Jaheez-iyeh from the girl's very birth, and most will certain-ly do so a long time before the daughter becomes of marrying age. Of course there is a Jaheeziyeh party as well (Jahaz-Boran), where the furnishings are (where space permits) presented and celebrated and where the bride and groom's new home and their future in

their new home is discussed.

Finally, the last major finan-cial step for the bride's family at this stage is to purchase the en-gagement and wedding band for the groom, and to host the Namzadi (engagement party).

Chapter 6:
Iranian Hospitality 101

My own immersion in all things Persian showed
me that Iranians have cultural habits which every
non-Iranian should learn – and learn as soon as pos-

sible, so as not to unintentionally raise any eyebrows. If you marry into an Iranian family, you'll probably learn all you need to know just by watching; a gentle clarification now and then from an Iranian friend will do the rest. But if you're a guest or even a vendor and you've never been to an Iranian home or attended Iranian ceremonies and parties, the last thing you want to do is offend, however inadvertently.

SHOES

When you enter an Iranian home, you will likely be asked to remove your shoes at the door or right outside before entering the home. There's no mystery why: once you enter a proper Persian home and see the magnificently beautiful hand-knotted silk Persian carpets on every floor, you won't even *think* about putting a dusty shoe on those gorgeous works of art.

GUESTS

Iranian people are serious about treating guests in their home with politeness – maximum politeness. Guests are honored in an Iranian home. Guests are always treated well, and there is an incredibly respectful, fun and playful exchange which occurs when an Iranian is hosting guests. This exchange of honor goes both ways. It was two years into dating my husband before I even realized that there were certain guests my in-laws

didn't get along with. You would never know it when those guests showed up. They were treated like kings and queens in my in-laws' home. Differences were set aside. Maximum politeness was given. Learn this lesson: do not ever use a home visit for wedding discussions, or any other sort of visit, to overtly gossip, make snide remarks, or be rude in an Iranian home.

IRANIAN GREETINGS

Greetings tend to be warm, and they tend to be lengthy. When a guest arrives and is greeted, a warm and loving exchange of sweet sayings in Farsi is typical. Some typical greetings are listed below.

Realize that you can go a long way in learning Farsi and in gratifying your Iranian hosts, just by knowing and practicing the simple greetings below. Remember too that greetings are lengthy. Just a short hello is acceptable, but if you're able to greet fluently by using two or three of the phrases below you'll make a great first impression.

Once you learn these simple greetings, you can slowly expand your vocabulary. Language study materials abound – you can almost certainly find them at the library or online. I personally recommend Pimsleur's Persian. They offer ten lessons on CDs on Amazon and iTunes). The lessons are simple, straightforward and useful – these are the phrases I use every single time I speak with Iranian people. The price is reasonable, less than $20.00 for the first 10 lessons. They're all you need to get started, and you can listen to them in the car too – which is how I learned!

Remember, though: attending a Persian wedding doesn't mean having to take a full foreign language course. All you really need is to master a few basics, for politeness' sake.

And when it comes to politeness, your Iranian hosts will show you more than you've ever seen in one place in your life. Be assured that any efforts to speak Farsi will be met with support, excitement and gentle approval, and help and understanding will be given all along the way.

HOW TO SAY "HELLO"

Salaam – Hello
Aloo - Hello

THREE WAYS TO SAY, "HOW ARE YOU?"

Chetori! (or) *Chetori?* – Short versions of "How are you?"
Khoob hasti? - "Are you doing well?"
Hale tun Khoob hast? - Literally "Is your health well?"

SIX WAYS TO SAY, "THANK YOU":
(Be fluent in Farsi thank-you's. You'll be saying them a lot!)
Merci - Thank You

Tashakor - Thank you

Mamnoon - Thank you

Kheli Mamnoon - Thank you very much (Many thanks)

Khaste Naboshie – literally, "I hope you are not tired!"
(A polite indirect way of saying thank you, as if to

say, "I hope you haven't exhausted yourself preparing this wonderful table, sharing this wonderful meal, etc.")

Daste Shoma Dard Nakoneh – literally, "I hope your hands don't hurt." (As in "I hope your hands don't hurt after all this work cooking, shopping, hosting, etc."

GIFT GIVING

It took me three years to realize that gift giving is almost mandatory when visiting an Iranian home.

From the first time I ever met my future mother-in-law to the last time I saw her a few weeks ago, there is always 100% of the time a gift waiting for me when I arrive. Always. Sometimes it's chocolates or perfume beautifully wrapped up. Other times, it is a lovely designer purse.

But gift-giving isn't unique to my dear mother-in-law. It's typical in Iranian culture. In Iranian culture, guests, friends and family are dearly treasured and loved and highlighting and reinforcing that love for one another in every imaginable way is common among Iranians. Parties, frequent gatherings, signs and tokens of respect, and, of course, gifts are normal.

So bringing a gift is customary. It isn't mandatory, exactly, but it would be like arriving in Court without your shoes or shirt. It's simply not done. The gifts need not be expensive! And you'll nearly always find yourself receiving gifts in return. But you need to understand the core meaning of the practice. The exchange is not intended to be a requirement or a burden; it is intended to be a sign of respect, honor, love and gratitude from giver to receiver. The key is for the gift to be thoughtful, considerate and symbolic. Of what? Respect, well-wishing and loving-kindness, these are truly gifts of love and should be thought of only in that way.

What are typical gifts? A small box of chocolates. Fruit in a basket. A small basket of flowers. Sweets (especially Persian sweets). Persian tea. Dried fruits

(Note: gifts marked by a personal touch, such as buying dried fruit and a small basket, and then arranging the fruit yourself on a small platter or in small bags tied with pretty ribbons are particularly well received.)

TAROF KARDAN, AKA "TAROFFING"

Iranians are famous for their Tarof Kardan. What's that? Something of a paradox, but one you have to really understand well if you plan on visiting an Iranian household. It is a paradox because although the intention of this conversational exchange is to make you unburdened and comfortable, if you don't understand what is going on, it is very uncomfortable!

Tarof Kardan refers to a conversational exchange between two people based on the exceptionally high standard of politeness and hospitality for which Iranians are well known. Think of it as exceptional attention being paid to your comfort. Above all Iranian hosts want their guests to be comfortable, unburdened, well fed and well cared for.

If for any reason they have the impression that this is not occurring, they will politely "Tarof" in order to make a guest more comfortable. Unfortunately, sometimes the effect is opposite and the guest becomes more uncomfortable than before! This generally occurs when you do not understand what is going on: a situation I was in many times myself in the past. Consider this example of Tarof Kardan that I personally experienced:

"A broken vase? Don't worry about it!"

At a dinner party at the home of my mother-in-law and father-in-law, a guest broke a vase. Needless to say, the guest felt terrible and immediately began picking it up and offering to replace it.

My mother-in-law and father-in-law laughed calmly and waved their hands, saying "That old thing! We've been trying to get rid of that for years. Thank you for helping us get rid of that thing."

What should you do, oh non-Iranian guest, if you find yourself unexpectedly caught in an exchange of Tarof Kardan with someone from Iran? Play along for a while. It's expected. And once you know that it's really a kind of game, it can actually be quite fun. But if you sense the minutes turning into hours and the fun beginning to drain away -- just give up! Your Tarof Kardan partner will be immensely gratified.

Iranian Good-Byes

Iranian farewells are even longer than the greetings. Why so long? Because you must say goodbye to absolutely everyone. Are a hundred or so family members there, down to the fourth cousin twice removed's spouse? Seek each one out personally and say goodbye to them, with all the politeness at your command. Once you finally head for the door, the hosts will be there to beg you to have more food, more tea or more sweets before you go. In fact, why don't you stay longer? There may even be gifts of food for you to take home. Once you've put your coat on, then of course you'll say goodbye again to everyone at the door. Perhaps you think that once you're outside the door, you're safe. Not even close. Pedram and I may be in our car in the street attempting to pull into the street. The good-byes are still in full swing! If you want to leave a Persian get-together early – well, give up. It won't happen. Just enjoy it to the full and expect a long departure time.

Saying Goodbye in Farsi

Khoda-hafez - Goodbye
Kheli khoshal shodam - It made me happy to see you!
Shab-be kheyr - Good night

Chapter 7:

Persian Party Dance Stamina and Attire

HOW TO FAKE IT TILL YOU MAKE IT IN GRAND STYLE

I love to dance. Doesn't everyone? For as long as I can remember, whenever my family would get together, the music would come on and the dancing would start. Iranians are exactly the same. When you're in a Persian home and the music starts to play, make room! You're about to see an immediate eruption of dancing, joy and fun.

Don't worry about not being expert. Iranians not only love Persian-style dancing, they love even attempts at Persian-style dancing, and any guest who even *tries* to Baba Karam will be treated to compliments that would make Fred Astaire, Mikhail Baryshnikov and Michael Jackson blush.

It's just one more example of boundless Persian

courtesy and of the boundless Persian delight in anyone who shows interest or takes joy in any aspect of Persian culture, including Persian dance.

HOW TO LEARN TO DANCE PERSIAN STYLE

Find someone who already knows. My teacher was my (much beloved) sister-in-law, Parisa. "It's all about the arms and hands, Christen!" she'd say, as we'd practice in her living room, twirling, weaving, dancing around, getting ready for the never-ending cascade of Persian parties, especially the endless celebrations around Nowruz, the Persian New Year. Parisa is a wonderful dancer, but just as every American knows how to throw a football or eat a hot dog, every Iranian knows how to dance. Find one and let them know you

want to dance Persian style too. They'll be delighted!

After that? One word. Mohammad Khordadian. This man is the Alpha and Omega of Persian Dance – a dancing guru of absolute genius who knows every move in the book and has added a few editions of his own! Mohammad Khordadian is the man. He has a

set of DVDs that will teach you all you need to know.

And best of all: go to Persian parties and just sit and watch. Trust me; people will start dancing sooner or later. When I was learning how to dance Persian style, I'd just sit, watch and copy the moves. Sometimes I'd join in and get delighted advice or practice at home until I had them all down right.

That's still how I do it!

PARTY STAMINA

Iranians know how to party. I mean, Iranians really know how to totally absolutely completely 100% capital-P *party*. They not only throw their heart into it, they toss in their skin, bones, circulatory system, and everything else in too! Their parties are high energy

undertakings that last all evening, all through the night and deep into the wee hours of the morning to boot. And those are just the informal parties. When you come to main events like Persian weddings, sheer stamina becomes a major consideration. My sister Courtney and her husband Kerry just plain ran out of steam during our Persian Wedding! They had to find a couch and stretch out to rest. Most Persian weddings end the next morning as breakfast is being served.

So, seriously, just know that you'll need stamina for these events. Prepare yourself: get some appropriate rest beforehand; realize that it might be a very late night even if it sounds like a simple dinner. It's a good idea to get some sleep during the day when you know you're going to an Iranian party at night and not to schedule any heavy appointments for early the next morning.

Because between the late night festivities and all the extended hellos, goodbyes, dancing, eating, Taroffing and Baba Karaming, you're in for a long night.

Iranians know this. When I visited Iran itself for the first time, one of the things I noticed (and loved) was that everything in the country seemed to

CHRISTEN FLACK BEHZADI, M. D.

close down in the middle of the day. Store owners and employees alike went home and rested. They had a meal with the family. They slept. Then, later in the day, they returned to work. Resting in the day provided the stamina I needed for all the evening dinner parties I attended in Iran.

As with so much else, this is one more item in the long Iranian list of how to live well. But if you're going to a major Iranian party, learn this one well. Get some rest before the party. You'll be glad you did when you're invited onto the dance floor again at 4 AM.

HOW TO DRESS

Don't be shy. That would be my best advice. Think gaudy. In dress as in dance, food and marathon partying, Iranians go the whole nine yards. Understated dress subtlety? Save it for job interviews. There's an American saying that sums up Persian party dress codes perfectly: if you got it, flaunt it. And often in Persian parties "got it" means Dolce & Gabana, Gucci, Chanel, Christian Louboutin – you get my drift. The Persians are known to have a particularly refined flair for fashion. Skip the flip-flops (even bedazzled ones) and the flats of all sorts. Just go for it.

And I would add, flaunt it everywhere. In American culture, highlighting one thing usually means downplaying other things. My instincts are that if I tend to don flashy earrings, the oversized necklace has to go, and the hair shouldn't call attention to itself either: the earrings are the centerpiece. I have learned, that's not the way Iranians tend to do things. They go for it! Dresses are bold. Hair is bold. Make-up and earrings and bangles and jewelry are super-bold. Throw in the kitchen sink – if it's Carerra marble with gold fixtures, engraved ivory inlays and Cupids! Take it to the max, and you'll still probably be considered a conservative dresser.

When I first went to Iran, I thought in the

back of my mind that I would probably be the stylish American girl in the veiled Middle East. It was the exact opposite. I had a feeling when we had arrived initially in Dubai and I saw a heavily veiled woman

in shoes I knew to be several thousand dollars and no less than 15 24-karat gold bangles on her arm. In Iran, it was no different. In fact, to my surprise, Tehran is like one big catwalk for men and women alike. I was worried about not being conservative enough in my dress (which was the furthest thing from the truth when I got there) but I did not have to worry- With the ultra-conservative wardrobe I packed I looked like a villager on the cat walk. I'm sure no one even noticed I was there. The women and their heels – at the market! – were towering. They were dressed impeccably in mid-day. It was

unbelievable to me how fashionable the Iranian people were as a whole. The women and their jewelry-oh my goodness! The jewelry was exquisite and all the women seemed drenched in it. I couldn't even pretend to keep up with the Iranian women. It was such a joy on my first visit to Iran. Paris and Tehran are my two favorite cities in the world to do some serious people watching.

If you think that this flair for fashion will get full expression at a Persian wedding, you are right. But there are some guidelines you need to know

Black is a good example of this. Persian women are famous both for their style and for their penchant for wearing black. Black is acceptable at Persian weddings, but is still somewhat taboo. You will almost never see the bride wearing black at a wedding event, but, it's fair game for guests.

This brings me to an important point. In the United States a guest wouldn't dare wear white to a wedding unless it was clearly stated as part of the dress code. White is reserved for the bride. Iranian weddings are different: it's entirely acceptable for female guests to wear white and such guests frequently do. However, if you're having a mixed-culture wedding, and an American bride and guests who absolutely expect white to be reserved for the bride, make it very clear in your invitations if you don't want guests wearing white.

And there's one more very important thing to remember. You're going to be dancing a lot and eating and drinking a lot. Wear clothing that feels comfortable enough to dance in and that compliments your figure if it becomes momentarily fuller. Skintight and buckled-up won't work – give yourself room to move and to breathe.

Part Two:

PERSIAN IMMERSION CAMP

AND

THE HISTORY OF THE PERSIAN WEDDING

Chapter 8:
The Persian Mother and Courtship Basics

THE PERSIAN MOTHER, THE DIFFERENT KINDS OF PERSIAN MARRIAGES, FAMILY MEETINGS & GREETINGS

THE PERSIAN MOTHER

Since I am writing this book from the perspective of those of us who "do not know what Persian means" let me just simply explain that the bond between Persian boys and their mothers tends to be very strong and very close. They don't just favor their mothers; they absolutely, unconditionally, adore, cherish and love their mothers. One of these days I will watch a Persian mother with her young son and take notes so I can figure out what to do to raise sons devoted to me well into adulthood!

Non-Iranian brides may be surprised to see how strongly Persian sons treasure their mothers. Let me share a few experiences of my own that illustrate that (and that illustrate its benefits, too). When I began dating my husband, I noticed immediately that he was extremely attentive to me. He seemed to be

very tuned into and used to caring for a woman. He had clear ideas that were fully developed about the adoration, commitment and respect that women deserved. He did not want me to be stressed-ever. To this day almost three years into our marriage, when my husband makes a to-do list #1 on his list every time is "Make sure *khoshie*[1] has an easy life."

This is the sign of a man who has grown up learning to

love, adore and respect women. My mother-in-law is my ally and I don't know what I would do without her.

1Khoshgel in Farsi means "beautiful." So my husband calls me Khoshgel, or "Khoshie" for short. As I said, these mamas raise their boys right!

Sometimes when your husband is "in a bad mood" or "had a bad day," they can on occasion bring that home. This can cause stress in the home. My husband is very easy going, but even he has tough days that are difficult to "shake off." When these days come and despite my best efforts, I cannot find the right words to calm, soothe and re-center my husband, I don't hesitate to call his mother. Without fail, he can speak to his mother and after their conversation he is re-centered, calmed and back to himself. As a wife, this is a great benefit. With that said, let us explore the different kinds of marriages in Iran.

THE TYPES OF IRANIAN MARRIAGES

There are two kinds of marriages in Iran; arranged and non-arranged. The first, increasingly rare, particularly outside Iran, is the arranged marriage put together by a matchmaker. Matchmakers are not sought out at soaring prices when this route is chosen. Make no mistake about it, an Iranian woman is a proficient, skilled and certified matchmaker by birth. And likewise female family members generally serve as surrogate matchmakers if this is desired. An arranged marriage will follow the formal steps outlined in the following chapters quite closely.

But, while not uncommon centuries ago, arranged marriages are no longer the rule, particularly in more modern or expatriate communities. There, the bride and groom will often meet and get to know each other in the simple course of living their everyday lives. Also (particularly in smaller or expatriate communities) members of the families of the bride and groom may well already know and like each other and socialize quite freely. Nonetheless, once it appears that marriage may unite existing friends into lasting family, tradition re-awakens and formalities and the courtship process will generally be respected and proceed through the expected stages. They may proceed in a more relaxed manner, and the goal may not be introduction and familiarization so much as an excuse to party and to honor genuinely beloved traditions; plus, of course, to work out the thousand-and-one details of the ceremonies, parties and the marriage arrangement itself.

Whether the couple and their families are strangers or friends, the steps that the bride, groom and their families will take to become one will nearly always follow traditional patterns and sequence. This is true even in modern times. Even if every event is not explicitly hosted, the tone of the sequence remains. So the goal of Part II is to familiarize you with the tone and sequence of the courtship events leading up to the proposal and engagement.

In Iranian culture, the meeting (Didar) and courtship (Ashnaei) of a couple is not something that involves them alone. The joining of the families is almost as much a part of the meaning of the union as the joining of the bride and groom. Indeed, in the very beginning of the marriage process, one can argue that families are perhaps even more involved.

Even today, inside Iran or outside, many Iranian mothers will seek out women from good families as potential brides for their sons.[4] But today, again both inside Iran or outside, women and men also meet at college, at work and in and around town.[5] So "getting to know you" family events are now often more casual "getting to know you better" family events. The edge may be taken off what might otherwise be hard-nosed negotiating events simply because discussions have already more or less, here and there, taken place informally. Informal understandings nonetheless need to be formalized at some point, and these formal, meaningful, purpose-driven events often heighten

---

[4]*Note that this only works one way. A mother might look for an appropriate bride for her son, but mothers do not seek men for their daughters. Iranian wedding customs are traditional and in that tradition men are the ones who court, honor, cherish and care for the women. Women have no obligation to "hunt" for men.*

[5]*Women actually out-number men in most Iranian Universities. A December 2011 BBC report recently stated that as many as 70% of the graduates of one university in Iran were women. Go, girls!*

and clarify the seriousness of wedded union, the understanding of what each will bring to the marriage and the compatibility of the couple.

And it must always be remembered that although a high-profile family presence is undoubtedly the case, and welcome at that, it is not the family that decides whether or not a marriage will take place. It is up to the couple themselves to choose whether or not they want to be married and commit their lives to one another.

It should also be remembered that while tradition is key in the Persian wedding ceremony, it isn't for the pure sake of tradition alone. It's because tradition is regal, romantic, elegant, suave – fun, in short. I don't happen to be Iranian at all, yet I love the traditionalism manifest in these events, the sheer intoxicating glamour and resonance of it all.

Those lucky enough to experience the courtship and dating phase of a Persian wedding will also have another wonderful surprise awaiting them. It is not only the potential groom who is courting you, his family, his parents and his friends are also doing so. Everyone will treat you like a princess; everyone will give you all the honors and respect due to you as a potential Persian bride.

Does it come at no price? I suppose that depends on each individual bride. Yes, every bride will experience an endearing and refreshing chivalry that will all but engulf her during these events. She may be so dazzled that she realizes intuitively that being treated like a princess requires that she, in turn, behaves like a lady, as my dear father would say. That goes without saying, but I mention it regardless, for completeness' sake. And also to remind non-Iranian brides that behaving like a lady

means to understand what is customary when it comes to Persian wedding attire, etiquette, gifts and manners. This book will help, but the principle is reciprocity: return unto others the kindness and courtesy that will be showered in abundance on you. Richly display all the lovely manners your parents taught you. Rest assured, they will fall on a most deserving and grateful audience.

But don't regard yourself as having to pass

muster or be on display. That's not the case at all. You should treat everyone like the elegant lady that you are because, after all, that is what you are; worth and courtesy should shine from you naturally.

But you're not there to demonstrate your worth and shower courtesy on them. They're there to demonstrate their worth and shower courtesy on you. At this stage, the purpose of these get-togethers is always for your potential husband-to-be and his entire family to put their best foot forward, show how very wonderful and worthy they are and to display their love and benevolence for the bride-to-be. She is a royal queen of the world whom they would be honored to have join their family. They are all suitors, and all asking for her gracious hand.

In Iranian culture, when a bride marries, she is said to leave her own family and join the groom's family. The groom's family becomes financially, emotionally and spiritually responsible for the bride to be and her well-being. If she accepts, she becomes not merely the wife of the groom, but a daughter to his parents and a new sister to his siblings. The separate families are not separate families any longer. When the couple is joined, the families are joined.

Needless to say, when the emotional stakes are so high and the consequences to their daughter and sister so dear, it goes without saying that the family of the bride will want to be certain that the groom is a good man and that the groom and his family are capable of emotionally and financially providing for her, however great her own resources and individual successes may be.

In this, an Iranian bride is – once again – uniquely blessed. An Iranian bride can be as strong, independent and successful as she pleases. But at the same time Iranian ways insist that the groom be financially and emotionally stable enough to provide for the bride

at all times. She can have it all, and at the same time the groom must be prepared to provide it all too. (Not surprisingly, Iranian unions tend to be prosperous ones.)

But before that union can take place, the groom's desire and ability to care for his bride, and to care for her very well indeed, must be absolutely demonstrated before an engagement can occur.)

Chapter 9:
Guests, Gifts, Attire and Manners

At this stage of the wedding process, even if you're "just going over for dinner" at your future in-laws' home, you're really not. They are showing you themselves at their very best, and while you are not absolutely required to do the same, the kindness and courtesy will be such that you'll find it all but impossible not to return their thoughtfulness. Keep love foremost in mind and the rest should take care of itself.

But study the guidelines below nonetheless, and keep them clearly in mind too – especially if both families are meeting formally for one of these events, and particularly if the events are one of the larger ones, such as the Baleh-boran, which on rare occasions can sprawl into an all-out mini-wedding to which hundreds are invited.

ATTIRE

Since everyone is putting their best foot forward, it goes without saying that those feet will appear inside the best shoes. Yes, formal tradition dictates formal attire. But strive for elegance – romantic elegance. Women should dress as though headed for their coronation and appear as the perfect royal princess the groom knows her to be. Grooms should dress at the height of fashion.

ETIQUETTE

Review Chapter 6 of this book – Persian Hospitality and then re-read it. Everything you will need to know is there. Follow every rule – and remember that following every rule to the letter without adding a touch of spirit is dead. Be on your very best manners but let them also radiate from the heart.

GIFTS

Again, see Chapter 6. There I discuss an appropriate gift for this stage. Suffice it to say that a groom

does *not* show up empty-handed to greet his potential bride to be and her family. This is no less true if you already happen to be dating. If anything, it's more true. Gentlemen, do not forget to bring a small gift for your future bride-to-be!

GUESTS

As the couple are getting to know each other, only close immediate family are invited, and there are serious discussions. As the couple nears a formal engagement, slowly more extended family and friends are invited and more and more discussions have resolved. At the engagement party (the Namzadi), the whole community is invited, and it may feel like the whole universe was invited too.

This is the end of discussions. It's time to party!

Chapter 10:
Didar and Ashnaei

THE MEETING AND COURTSHIP OF THE COUPLE

DIDAR AND ASHNAEI

Ashnaei is the period of courtship – the way in which a couple gets to know each other. Didar is the Farsi word meaning "to meet." So in the traditional Persian courtship process, a couple will have a chance to meet (Didar) and then gradually become better and more intimately acquainted (Ashnaei).

In earlier times, this process was far more formalized, with particularly heavy involvement in the details of the meeting by the families of the couple. Even today it is a given in Iranian culture that the families of the prospective bride and groom assess both the couple and each other to be sure the union will be a good match for the families as well as the couple.

In Iran itself, traditional parents still have a significant say in who their children marry. Of course

there are parts of modern-day Iran where men and women meet as they do in the West and simply begin dating out of pure attraction to one other. But in older times, the match-making process would involve mothers assessing local women as suitable prospects for their sons and families meeting and speaking with each other first before even allowing the potential couple to meet. Today you'll often find a mixture of old ways and new. Couples may meet and fall in love the modern way, but once a marriage appears to be in the making, tradition re-awakens and talks with family must follow before all parties are satisfied.

Chapter 11:
Khastegari

THE SUITOR AND THE MEETING OF THE FAMILIES

HAVING A KHASTEGARI

Khastegar is Farsi for the suitor; in other words, Khastegari is the coming of the suitor (the khastegar) to meet with the potential bride.

But the Khastegari is also a meeting between families and implies nothing but an interest in a serious relationship between the khastegar and the girl. The meeting is an opportunity for families of both the khastegar and the girl to convene and discuss a potential engagement and implies no commitment. The families have simply come to decide whether the khastegar and the girl would be a good couple and have arranged a meeting to explore the situation further.

In some instances, the khastegar and the girl may have already been dating or spoken with each other. They may want to pursue an engagement for reasons all their own. In such cases, Khastegari confers a new seriousness upon the relationship, and,

in proper Persian style, serves notice to the families involved.

But many practical things must be worked out between the two families before they can consider the prospect of marriage between the girl and the khastegar. Before, when marriages were arranged, it was the families who arranged the Khastegari meeting; now, in times when the bride and groom are free to date, they may arrange their own Khastegari as an opportunity for the families to meet and openly discuss issues relevant to the marriage.

The purpose of this first meeting is simply introductions, and, perhaps, preliminary negotiations; and nearly always it is the khastegar and/or his family that initiates it. Its purpose is simple. The khastegar and his family need to know everything they can about the bride before a decision is made to formally ask for her hand. The Khastegari takes place with that purpose in mind.

THE KHASTEGARI – THEN AND NOW

Historically, Iranian marriages were arranged. During Khastegari the khastegar's family would make a particularly detailed (though friendly) set of inquiries about the bride. Specifically, the khastegar and his family would be interested in meeting and getting to know the bride; they want to know about her education, her occupation, her family and whatever else the bride might be bringing to the marriage, should the couple decide to unite. The tone could be anything from great excitement to one of intense hard negotiation, all to ensure compatibility between the groom and the bride – and their families.

Today, as men and women more freely meet and date beforehand, this event becomes far more of a meeting between the families involved so that they can casually discuss matters related to marriage; the days of tough negotiating are almost entirely gone. But the event still centers on the khastegar making the decision whether or not to ask the girl to marry him. And so it places no small amount of pressure on the bride and her family to make a very good impression indeed on the khastegar and his family. Given the intense closeness evident in Persian culture, the families also want to know if they are a good match as a whole. From their perspective they will be very close and want to ensure a harmonious relationship so they may all support the couple fully.

What actually happens? At one time the Khastegari was divided into two parts, but these days the process takes place in one encounter. The prospective groom comes to the home of the bride with his family, and there formally presents himself as a khastegar, or the suitor, for the girl's hand. (On occasion, a friend or representative of the groom may come in the suitor's place.) The girl and her family happily welcome the prospective groom and his family into their home. The prospective bride is dressed superbly, and it is always she who opens the door for the khastegar and his family when they arrive.

The prospective bride is generally exceptionally polite and happily welcomes them to her family's home. The groom's family will then present small gifts, flowers and sweets and the like, to the potential bride and her family. (Jewelry and similar higher-end gifts are reserved for the engagement and beyond.)Many family members of both families are present – siblings, grandparents, aunts, uncles and cousins. Everyone greets everyone else with colorful welcome, joy and happiness. The khastegar's family are offered the best seats in the home (as any guest in a Persian home would be, really, but more warmly and extravagantly).

An important point is reached when the bride's father says: "Let the tea be served." The potential bride is closely observed as she pours the tea for the guests and offers them sweets, fruits and nuts. An elder of either family begins to speak and the discussions begin. The groom's family enquires about practical things, such as the education and background of the girl, her future plans, her hobbies and interests and especially her ideas about marriage.

In Persian wedding celebrations, the bride's family is responsible for the Jaheeziyeh[1], which are items purchased for the couple's future home.

[1]See chapters 5 and 17 for further information about the Jaheeziyeh.

Carpets, beds, things for the kitchen and so on, are traditionally purchased for Jaheeziyeh.

The groom's family will want to know what sort of Jaheeziyeh the prospective bride will be bringing, and they may (if they wish) negotiate for more items.

The bride's family will have questions too – but not too many at this stage; not at the Khastegari. The khastegar and his family are the honored guests and their comfort and concerns stand foremost. So the khastegar and the girl may be given a few moments together privately to speak to one another about themselves and their feelings without the pressure of family.

But overall the occasion is gregarious and social rather than intimate. The khastegar and his family are hosted for several hours of good conversation, gracious manners and fine eating which may well include a full dinner. Then the khastegar and his family leave and discuss the potential marriage privately, as a family.

If they're not interested in asking for the bride's hand in marriage, they'll let the bride's family know soon enough. And if the Khastegari does not work out (which is not uncommon), there are no hard feelings between families.

But what if the Khastegar is interested in the

girl, and the family does give its tacit approval? Then arrangements are made for another meeting: the Baleh-boran.

In Baleh-boran, the khastegar will formally ask for the girl's hand in marriage. But now it's the suitor's turn to go through a set of intensive inquiries into what he will bring to the marriage and to get the approval of the prospective bride's parents before he can ask her to marry him.

Baleh-boran, then, is the opportunity of the bride's family to look closely and deeply at the groom, his character and his prospects and ask what he will bring to the marriage. Baleh-boran is also the occasion when the bride's family actively negotiates on behalf of the girl, to make sure that the prospective husband brings quite enough to the union to ensure the bride's financial independence and comfort as well.

Incidentally, the groom is not the only one to bring gifts during the Baleh-boran. It's common for the groom's parents also to bring gifts for the bride. Traditionally, they say, this was done in order to better entice the potential bride to accept the groom. The gifts given during this ceremony may include a single piece of cloth for sewing a gown or in more modern times jewelry for the bride.

Chapter 12:
Baleh-Boran

THE GROOM WILL PROPOSE AT BALEH-BORAN

With Notes on Shrini Khoran

WHAT IS THE BALEH-BORAN?

"Baleh" is the Farsi word for "yes"; and the entire Baleh-boran revolves around the supreme moment when the possible bride-to-be looks at the potential groom-to-be and says to him, "Yes – I will marry you."

But the richness of the Baleh-boran process is far more intricate – and much more fun – than that simple question and answer.

Like the Khastegari, of which the Baleh-boran is in many ways a natural extension, the Baleh-boran serves several purposes, not least of which is a deepening of the familiarity between the respective families of the potential bride and groom. Every marriage is individual and concerns primarily the individuals who are marrying; but as you've probably learned by now, Persian marriages seem at times to be as familial as they are personal, as much a public event as a private union. It can often appear as though not just a madly in love couple but whole clans have come together to merge and feel one another out and (of course) party, which is what makes this stage and every stage of a Persian wedding, such a joy.

However, the Baleh-boran also raises the stakes and deepens the intimacy as well as the commitment between the parties. It is a further meeting that continues the ongoing negotiations between families, but one that also now takes it to a higher level of seriousness. In the same way, it is another opportunity for the candidate groom (the khastegar) and his intended to meet, but not only that: now it further allows the groom and his possible bride-to-be to talk about their potential marriage in private. In short, it is the moment when possibility crystallizes into reality, when romantic dreams take on form and become fact: the moment when the groom formally proposes marriage and is formally accepted or turned down. It is the beginning or the end.

And what if everything goes well? Then the Baleh-boran will ultimately lead to the even more ecstatic celebrations of the Namzadi – the official engagement party – or the Shirini-Khoran – a formal courting period with a promise to be married.

The Parent's Gifts

In some traditions, one elegant touch in the Baleh-boran is that the groom's parents often give gifts to the bride. Small gifts are a part of almost every wedding-ceremony-related meeting, of course, and are generally intended to convey a message as much as to present a gift. The message here is that the groom's parents accept and welcome the bride and wish to entice acceptance of the bride and her family to definitely accept the groom. The parent's gifts in this instance may be small, symbolism being the main object, but it's not uncommon for a touch of gift-giving extravagance to develop at this point, particularly if things have gone well and it seems that the bride's acceptance is now all but certain.

NEGOTIATIONS

Like all events leading up to the wedding, the Baleh-boran is hosted in the prospective bride's home. The khastegar and his family are, again, politely welcomed into the home of the bride for another meeting. Again, many family members of both families are present, including elders. Close friends of either family may also be attending.

But only very close friends this time: compared to other Persian wedding events, the Baleh-boran and the Khastegari are somewhat private. The reason is that, while it is generally expected that the meetings between all parties involved will turn out well, negotiations between families do on occasion fail and marriage does not take place. In the event that things do not work out, the families, naturally, would not want anyone sharing the perhaps uncomfortable details with the entire community. Hence less-than-close friends of the family (or known gossips) are rarely invited. Also generally excluded from these events are girls who may steal the attention of the khastegar and – of course – anyone not wishing the couple well.

But you'd be mistaken to think of the Baleh-boran as being stiff or legalistic. Its tone and spirit are nearly always bright and happy. After all, acceptance is considered likely at this point, particularly if the Khastegari has gone well. So a happy outcome – a glowing happiness – is anticipated. After all, the khastegar and his family have already visited, they have been pleased with what they have seen and they have now explicitly stated their interest in the potential bride. Both parties at this point would very much like the Baleh-boran to go well and see the couple pass into a formal engagement. So as to ensure that engagement does in fact come about, at the Baleh-boran, a confident groom and his family enter into the supportive and welcoming home of the potential bride, and all strive to be as polite and likable as possible and to show their very best behavior.

But however charming and polite the khastegar may be, before he can formally ask for the girl's hand in marriage, the bride's family must discuss what the khastegar can contribute to his potential bride – not just emotionally but financially.

THE MARIYEH (DOWRY)

In Persian culture, once the bride leaves her family and marries, she joins the groom's family. As such, the groom and his family are expected to provide and care for her. The Baleh-boran is an opportunity for the bride's family to understand the capacity of the groom and his family to care for their beloved daughter and to gauge the depth and sincerity of his intention to care for her. Before they can bless a marriage between the khastegar and their daughter, the bride's family must know the feelings and be assured of the honor and integrity of the khastegar and his family; they must be certain that their daughter will be cherished and live a life free from want. Before any engagement can take place, this must be definitely established. The Baleh-boran is where this is done.

One of the first considerations to come up is the Mariyeh. It's expected that a Persian groom will provide a Mariyeh for his bride – which is to say, a dowry, sometimes referred to as "the gift for love." This is the bride's security should the marriage not work out; so it is, as it were, non-refundable. At this event, both families will discuss the amount or nature of the Mariyeh, and at this time the costs involved with the wedding festivities, guest lists and events are discussed too. It is the groom who pays for the expenses of the wedding. So the bride's family will want to clearly know what financial contributions he is prepared to make in that regard as well.

The bride's family will not only ask the groom many questions about his financial status and intentions – in detail, they may even negotiate with the groom and the groom's family in regard to the items for which the groom will be responsible, should the couple engage and marry.

It should be pointed out that providing such a

security as the Mariyeh does not mean that the groom endows the bride and her family with significant funds on the spot. The Mariyeh ensures that the bride will

have means to live comfortably if and when the marriage ends, but it does not commit the groom to provide it all at once immediately. Persian weddings can indeed be lavish affairs, rich in gifts and festivities, but just as wonderful traditional marriages need not be impossibly costly, assuring a bride's financial future does not require immediate massive expenditures. If the groom owns a fine house in his own name, for example, he may during the Baleh-boran agree to put it in his wife's name. A high up-front cost expenditure is not necessarily required from the groom; assuring the financial safety and security of the bride is.

But the Baleh-boran is far from an exclusively monetary discussion. The bride's family simply

wants to be complete-
ly assured that the
groom is capable of
supporting the bride,
and that he is deter-
mined to support her
and cherish her. They
want to be assured
that he will not only
be kind and gentle,
but generous and
supportive of their
daughter before they
give him permission
to ask for her hand.

And although
the Baleh-boran and
the Khastegari are to
some degree meet-
ings centered on
finance, detail and
negotiations, neither
event is intended to
be a tense or overly
demanding encounter for either party. On the contrary! Both are a very special moment in the life of the
Iranian bride and groom: they and their two families

are joining together and uniting with one another as they elaborate the details of formalizing and celebrating the joyous union of the bride and groom in marriage. The financial details are merely the dressing; the love of the couple and their complete commitment to one another is the cake.

Persian culture is extremely respectful, hospitable and polite. Yet joy and celebration are encouraged at every turn, particularly when the event that sparks it is as intrinsically joyous as a marriage. So at the Baleh-boran, as at the Khastegari, guests to the bride's home are treated to the best of everything that the hosts have to offer. The bride's family wants to ensure that the khastegar and his family are as comfortable as it is possible to be during the negotiating events. The Baleh-boran is anything but a burden; as a rule it's extremely enjoyable. Why? Because if the couples and families already know each other informally, both generally already have an informal sense of each others' rough financial situation too; negotiations are already somewhat informed and more than somewhat friendly. On the other hand, if the marriage is arranged, the matchmaker arranging it has assessed both parties' financial picture beforehand. In both cases, it is far more a matter of clarifying details and understandings than of starting and finishing high-level legalistic negotiations from scratch.

The negotiations confirm explicitly what both parties more or less already know and more or less already expect; at which point – on with the party!

But it's party time with a practical purpose. Clear and open discussions are necessary if both families are to explicitly understand the mutual expectations of both families as to marriage and the marriage ceremony.

A PRIVATE TIME FOR THE COUPLE

Once the financial negotiations are done, and it is clearly established what expenses the khastegar's family will be responsible for and what expenses the bride's family will be responsible for, then comes the time for the girl and the khastegar to meet privately.

In private the two will discuss the details just gone over in the general family conversations, but this will be their opportunity to also discuss in private, neither family nor finance, but rather their feelings for each other and their expectations regarding their coming marriage.

Before the bride and groom meet privately, the girl's family will give their blessing to the khastegar to ask for her hand in marriage. Then both families will retire to another room and wait as the khastegar and the girl discuss by themselves the details of the meetings up to that point and their inner thoughts and feelings.

Even at this point, there is still no obligation to become engaged, and if the khastegar and the girl do not feel compatible, it is still perfectly acceptable for either party to politely decline. But that is rare. Especially nowadays, when the bride and groom have often already met and courted each other.

The Baleh-boran is not a mere formality; rather it is the placing of a seal on the couple's love for one another and on their intention to become one. Once the Baleh-boran occurs and the khastegar and the girl have discussed everything and are both satisfied, then the preliminaries are at an end. The process of becoming man and wife begins.

But first the private talk between the khastegar and his intended bride must take place. And when it does, and all appears well, what then? Then and there the suitor asks for her hand in marriage.

ANNOUNCING THE ACCEPTANCE

If the bride is happy with the khastegar and does indeed agree to marry him, they are not at that point formally engaged; but they are so much closer to it that celebration follows almost immediately. If the bride has a younger female family member, the girl will often be summoned to deliver the news. The girl will joyously emerge and tell the entire family that the bride-to-be has said "baleh!" – yes! – at which point immense cheering and celebration erupts. The families happily congratulate the couple and each other as the khastegar and his potential bride emerge from their private moment together. Everyone gives many a heartfelt "Mobarak!" (Congratulations) to each other as well as the happy couple, and the atmosphere is lively, ecstatic and celebratory.

The families will now begin to prepare for either a Shirini-Khoran – "eating of the sweets" – party; or for the official Namzadi – the engagement party.

SHIRINI-KHORAN OR NAMZADI?

Shirini-Khoran is Farsi for "eating of the sweets." The very traditional purpose of Shrini-Khoran dates back to the time of arranged marriages. In those times, when the families of a potential couple had decided a perfect match had been made then, of course, a party would ensue to formally promise a future marriage between the couple. The potential groom's family would show up to the potential bride's home with fabric to make a dress (or chador), a ring and sweets. The ring was a promise ring-a promise to be married when the couple was ready. There would also be feeding of the sweets "Shirini-Khoran" during this meeting as well. This meant if another khastegar's family came knocking on the door, the girl's family would tell them she has had a "Shirini-Khoran" and they would know she has promised to marry

someone else's son. Then the couple would have all the time they needed to grow up, finish their education, ensure financially stability and get to know each other better before getting married.

A more modern interpretation of the Shirini-Khoran is to allow for a formal courtship period. During the Shirini-Khoran, there is a formal commitment made between the bride and groom to enter into a courtship period. In this event, the bride and groom state their mutual intention to become engaged – or, perhaps to put it more precisely, to publicly become an officially engaged couple.

But the Shirini-Khoran has its limits. It must be remembered that the Shirini-Khoran is not a formal engagement; rather, it is a way for the couple to decide whether or not they want to become formally engaged. If the couple is certain about their union, there may not be a Shirini-Khoran at all: they may step directly to the next step: Namzadi (Engagement party). The Shirini-Khoran is declared only if the bride feels she needs more time to decide whether she is truly interested in the khastegar. This is identical to young American adults giving each other promise rings that they intend to be married in the future.

But the true goal does not change. The bride and groom use this time and opportunity to get to know each other in more depth and to decide whether they would genuinely like to be engaged and to marry. For although the bride may say "baleh" during the Baleh-Boron, that commitment is not irreversible. She can choose to enter into a formal courtship period to decide if she really wants to be married to the khastegar. If she decides she does not want to marry during the course of the Shirini-Khoran that is entirely acceptable.

EATING THE SWEETS

In earlier times, the Shirini-Khoran and the Namzadi (the official engagement party) were quite distinct stages in the marriage process. These days the Shirini-Khoran is often combined with the Namzadi in a ceremony involving the eating of the sweets. In such cases, the bride and groom simply feed each other sweets to acknowledge and honor the traditional Shirini-Khoran, but instead of entering into an official courtship period, they decide not to wait: they become formally engaged on the spot. As an acknowledgement of tradition (and as a charming way to indulge in sweets), having the bride and groom feed each other sweets is a simple, fun and elegant touch to add to Namzadi.

FROM BALEH-BORAN TO NAMZADI

The day of the Namzadi, or the day of the combined Shirini-Khoran and Namzadi, will be the day when the bride and groom officially become engaged. So it goes without saying that these events must be planned in advance. The Khastegari and Baleh-boran are smaller, more casual, more family-oriented events. From this point on though, events and celebrations become larger, more public (I nearly wrote, "more riotous!") and certainly more community-oriented.

And for those of you who are actually planning a Persian wedding? Celebrate too! Because the end of the Baleh-boran is the exciting moment where making your own Persian wedding come true officially begins! Starting with the Namzadi (engagement party) which is known to be as large and lavish as the wedding itself.

Chapter 13:

Namzadi

Namzadi is the engagement party where the couple is officially announced as being engaged (Namzadi) in front of the entire community. This is a very public event. The commitment, the negotiations and the preliminaries involving the families and the couple have all been made. Now it is time to let the world know with a grand party!

THE CEREMONIAL PART OF NAMZADI

The Namzadi only has two ceremonial parts to it – the exchanging of rings and the feeding of the sweets. The groom and bride each give the other a ring during the Namzadi. The rings are typically plain. (The bride receives the more expensive jeweled ring at the wedding.)

The couple will then feed each other sweets. This is called Shirini-Khoran (literally in Farsi: "Eating of the sweets"). Any Persian sweet will do for this portion of the ceremony. The couple feed each other sweets, but the sweet is a symbol too: a physical surrogate for the thought and intention of a sweet life together in marriage and throughout all their life together .

THE NAMZADI PARTY

The Namzadi party is an elaborate party. The bride will be dressed up beautifully, wearing a dress as fancy as the final wedding dress, but generally in a different soft color like pistachio or pink; and she will be as well-dressed if the family invites 30 guests as she will be if they invite 300 guests (and it is common for Namzadi to be as large as the wedding).

The Namzadi will have and be literally everything that a wedding would have and be – a large feast, entertainment, dancing, beautiful drapery and colorful décor – the works! The Namzadi is lavish, and the family of the bride will host and pay for the Namzadi.

But the purpose and beauty of Namzadi is not

purely a matter of a lavish budget or of how lengthy the guest list may be. The purpose of the Namzadi is to announce that the couple has chosen to marry and to celebrate that choice – in as grand a fashion as so grand a moment requires.

"Dear God,
Let all lovers be content,
Give them happy endings,
Let their lives be a celebration,
Let their hearts dance in the
fire of your love."

— *Jalal al-Din (Rumi)*

Part Three:

Pre-Wedding Events & Preparations

Shopping, Preparation
& More Celebrations

Chapter 14:
Pre-Wedding Shopping

Once the couple is engaged, the first order of business is to shop for the first few items of the wedding table.

ITEMS FOR THE WEDDING TABLE

On their wedding day, the bride and groom sit at a wedding table covered with an elaborate symbolic spread of items. This is called the Sofreh Aghd and it is in some ways the centerpiece of the wedding ceremony, almost more than the actual ceremony itself.

This isn't in the least to downplay the importance of the ceremony. It's just that the wedding ceremony is what occurs; the Sofreh Aghd tells you why it is occurring. The Sofreh Aghd is a breathtakingly spectacular symbolic jewel filled with the loving thoughts, intentions and deeds of the person who prepared it especially for the couple. It is anything but a random collection of knick-knacks. It is far closer in meaning to – and really is – a work of art.

Needless to say, the preparation of such an exceptional thoughtful and meaningful statement is quite an undertaking and great and long attention must be given to it. A grand Persian wedding with a poor Sofreh Aghd is unthinkable. The next chapter will discuss each item on the wedding table and its meaning. Each item is deeply symbolic for the couple – each item radiates a small specific heartfelt wish for something good for the couple.

For good luck, the couple should purchase the first three items of the Sofreh Aghd together.

The first item is the Holy Book. The Holy Book is purchased first – and it need not be just one Holy Book. If the couple holds separate religious views, a Holy Book representing the faith of each is more than acceptable. It is perfectly fine for the Torah to sit beside the Q'uran or the Book of Mormon to sit beside the Dhammapada. Again, the Persian wedding is not a religious ceremony unique to any one religion:

it is a cultural ceremony, but one that wisely and honestly acknowledges – and celebrates – the religious elements of the cultures from which the bride and groom spring.

The Holy Book or Holy Books are there for multiple reasons, but one is to honor the faith of both the bride and the groom. If there is more than one faith to be honored, that is perfectly acceptable and entirely welcome: both are honored without reserve.

And both are seen as honoring and sharing certain fundamentals: for instance, either Holy Book on the wedding table symbolizes God and the importance of prayer in the marriage. The reason that the Holy Book or Holy Books are purchased first is that the couple in their hearts are asking for God's permission to be married.

The second item to be purchased is the mirror.

The mirror symbolizes absolute truth. In a mirror, what you see is what you get. The early purchase of the mirror symbolizes the couple's commitment to truthfulness and honesty with one another throughout their marriage.

Finally, two candelabra are purchased. The fire from the candles represents purity and light and a wish for all the beauty in life that springs from purity and light.

ITEMS FOR THE BRIDE-TO-BE

The groom purchases the bride's wedding gown. He also purchases her wedding shoes. You would imagine that a smart groom will certainly send his mother with the bride as she chooses her gown and allow her to cover the costs at the time of purchase. However, sometimes there is a rather fun game common to Iranian culture involving the bride's wedding shoes.

Here's how it works. The groom goes and purchases the shoes for his bride for the wedding – alone. (A man purchasing a woman's shoes without her being present? Incredible but true.) Then the brave buyer sends the shoes to the bride at home. She opens the package and tries a shoe on. If the shoe fits perfectly, then everyone – what else? – celebrates, because it

means that they will be a "perfect fit" together. But if the shoe is small, the couple will struggle; and if it is large, then the couple will have a rocky road involving many ups and downs. So here's wishing that all brides have a perfectly fitting shoe from their groom!

And with these gifts in place, you now proceed to one of the most important chapters of this book and to one of central highlights of the Persian wedding: the Sofreh Aghd.

Chapter 15:
The Sofreh Aghd

THE SOFREH AGHD
(THE WEDDING TABLE)

CHAPTER 15

THE SOFREH AGHD

Items of The Sofreh Aghd

The Mirror
The Candelabra
The Holy Book(s)
Flowers
The Silk Cloth (Termeh)
Honey
Yoghurt
Rock Candy
Bread, Cheese, Green Herbs
Fruit
Flatbread (Mobarak Baad)
A Tray of Seven Spices
The Seven Colors of Espand
Seven Colored Threads and a Needle
Gold Coins
Rosewater
Nuts
Sweets
Noghl
Eggs
Two Sugar Loaves
The Cloth Held Over The Couple
The Table Cloth
The Chairs for The Couple

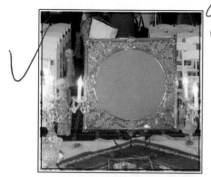

got it mine

THE MIRROR

The Mirror incarnates light and truth. It is positioned directly in line with the couple, and their reflection in the mirror radiates the light of their love back to them.

got it. (2) crystal A.D. need Candles!

THE CANDELABRA

The Mirror symbolizes not only light but fire — not destructive fire, but fire that burns away the transient and leaves only that which is eternal - such as the love of the wedding couple.

THE HOLY BOOK(S) *Cathy get Stand*

A Holy Book or Books symbolizes the presence and blessing of God. Just as God's universe includes different faiths, the Sofreh Aghd may include different books.

FLOWERS

Traditionally the floral arrangements are positioned in parallel on each side of the central mirror. Both sides should either match or harmonize beautifully.

2 large GOLD Milan Vases

Christen Flack Behzadi, M. D.

TERMEH: THE SILK CLOTH

The Termeh is a beautifully hand-woven silk or wool cloth, a product of ancient Persian art. It is often directly made in Iran, and sometimes used as a prayer rug, symbolizing submission to God.

HONEY

Honey describes the sweetness of the situation and the many wishes for a sweet life shared by the bride and groom.

Small vases A.D.

Same style Vase For below →

YOGHURT

Yoghurt symbolizes good health. But it is also an item that appears on almost every table where Iranians dine.

Small BiAs Bowl ## ROCK CANDY

Rock candy is another symbol of life's sweetness and love's sweetness, and the rock-like crystal is said to express hopes for a particularly enduring sweetness.

BREAD, CHEESE, GREEN HERBS

The white cheese represents purity; the bread, the staff of life; green herbs, good health. Together all express the wish for luck and health for the couple through basics, fundamentals, foundations.

FRUIT *Large Bias Bowl*

Fruit is a given, but apples, grapes and pomegranates in particular are mandatory. All fruits represent good health, but the three above are "the heavenly fruits," mentioned by Muhammad and in Jewish and Christian scripture.

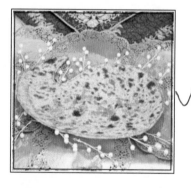

'MOBARAK BAAD' FLATBREAD *my 2 clock*
gold holder

Bread symbolizes prosperity and good health – the bread of life. But there is always at least one fkatbread with "Congratulations" (in Farsi, "Mobarak Baad") written on it with seeds.

A TRAY OF SEVEN SPICES

The 7 spices protect the couple from the "Evil Eye," and drive away evil spirits (and bad vibes in general).

TALLEST FOOTED CYLINDER VASE

Christen Flack Behzadi, M. D.

THE SEVEN COLORS OF ESPAND

Espand (wild rue) seeds, in seven colors, are thrown over burning coals, and the smoke which arises from the coals neutralizes any negativity around the couple.

SEVEN COLORED THREADS (AND
A NEEDLE)

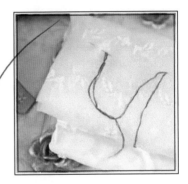

Seven threads, because seven is lucky, and colored threads are colorful; the needle is there to add the threads to a swathe of sheer fabric held over the couple.

GOLD COINS

Gold coins symbolize wealth and prosperity — and to save rather than spend them is both wise and customary.

ROSEWATER

Rosewater has a long history of use as a perfume, and one often used in Eastern Orthodox, Hindu, Zoroastrian and Muslim religious ceremonies.

NUTS *long stemmed* ~~Short cylinder vase~~ *vase*

Nuts are a symbol of abundance and renewal, and represent the wish that there will always be healthy food in the home of the couple.

SWEETS

"Life is sweet," and sweets stand for the sweetness of love, of life, of friendship, of family, of celebration, or marriage, of the past and the future, and of everything good that is or has been or is to come.

NOGHL *mis piece*

The Persian sweet. Noghls are to Iranians what hot dogs are to Americans, wine is to the French, or coffee is to office workers. No reception, or Sofreh, is conceivable without it.

EGGS *Rglity Bowl*

Eggs represent fertility and express hopes for a fruitful marriage, strong and healthy children, and a long and honorable lineage.

CHRISTEN FLACK BEHZADI, M. D.

TWO SUGAR LOAVES

The sugar loaves are rubbed together over a fabric held over the bride and groom's heads, sprinkling a snowfall of sweetness onto the veil and, by implication, over the couple.

THE CLOTH HELD OVER THE COUPLE

A sheer fabric is held over the couple, to catch sugar from the sugar loaves. Afterwards it is placed on the table, often holding the needle with seven colored threads.

Provided by Sima?

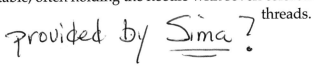

THE TABLE CLOTH

The table cloth is the backdrop for the entire Sofreh. It is nearly always white, symbolizing purity.

*Provided by BBJ linen
decide on size needed*

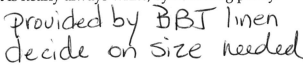

THE CHAIRS FOR THE COUPLE

The wedding couple has special seats especially assigned to them at the Sofreh Aghd. Symbolically, it is not too much to consider them thrones.

2 Crush benches white

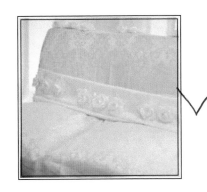

THE SOFREH AGHD

The wedding table (sometimes called the wedding spread) known in Farsi as the Sofreh Aghd is the quintessential centerpiece of all the wedding festivities. Mothers dream their entire life of preparing the wedding table for their children, and little girls dream of the day they too will be sitting at their own sparkling wedding table with all of its loving symbolism shining before them.

This wedding table is custom-prepared especially for each couple. The couple will sit at special seats at the head of the wedding table during the ceremony. And typically there will be 24 symbolic items almost always present on each wedding table (plus or minus a few items which each couple can tailor to their own tastes).

These items of the Sofreh Aghd contain profound meaning for the bride and groom. The central message at the core of all such items on the Sofreh Aghd is the sweetest and kindest wishes imaginable: wishes for happiness, luck, prosperity, health and closeness to God. The items are permeated with love from the family and friends of the couple and are intended to radiate every goodness it is possible to conceive toward the loving couple. It is indeed the dazzling centerpiece of the Persian Wedding.

Persian weddings – particularly cross-cultural Persian weddings – are nothing if not flexible and creative, a joy and an art. But there are few things that are an absolute requirement. Among them are the Sofreh Aghd. If you plan to have a Persian wedding, you will have to plan your Sofreh Aghd – and a darned fine one! A well-planned and well-done Sofreh Aghd will include each of the following items, which you will have to acquire and place on the actual wedding spread.

The meaning of the items, and their Farsi names, follows. Learn them: because the guests are sure to fall over themselves praising the quality, appropriateness and thought you obviously lavished on each. When choosing the items, also always remember the theme you have chosen. (The 'theme'? Stay with me; I'll explain shortly.)

Remember that the size of your Sofreh Aghd must comfortably accommodate the items so that there are no yawning gaps or any empty (khali) areas. Remember, items are never crammed, never spread haphazardly and never sitting apart. The goal, as with the marriage, is a well-integrated, lovingly attentive, harmony.

The start of this chapter gave you a quick list of all 24 items; here they are again, with more in-depth information about the symbolism and significance of each.

THE MIRROR

Ayaneh

The mirror sits at the very head of the wedding table. It is not a passing purchase – flowers at the wedding table may fade, sweets may be eaten, but the Ayaneh will stay with the couple forever. Once the wedding is over, the mirror is generally placed on display in the home of the couple, and it remains a treasured possession all of their lives.   W h y such importance? Because of its meaning and its symbolism; the Ayaneh incarnates light. The Ayaneh is positioned directly in line with the couple as they sit at the opposite end of the wedding table, and their reflection in the mirror radiates the light of their love back to them.

The mirror also represents another sort of light – the light of truth. What you see in the mirror is what you get: it therefore represents honesty, reality, purity – that which is. And that which is, is the love of this singular, individual couple, displayed before the world, their community and God and is confirmed in the mirror.

Traditionally the bride enters the room veiled. The groom looks not at her but at the Ayaneh as she removes her veil. The first thing he sees in the mirror should be the reflection of his wife-to-be.

CHRISTEN FLACK BEHZADI, M. D.

The Candelabra

Shamdoon

Like the mirror, candelabra carry the symbolic weight of light, but also the symbolic weight of fire. In the Zoroastrian world-view, fire is not a destructive agent but a purifying one, bringing illumination and removing all that which merely passes and all that is transient, leaving only that which endures and is eternal – such as the love of the bride and the groom.

There are always, and only, two candelabra, and they need not be exact duplicates, though they often are. Candelabra may shine with electric light, not candle light – ours, pictured here did. (Electric or candle, however, the candelabra, the mirror, and the next item, the Holy Book or Books, are always the first three items purchased, traditionally and for good luck.)

Not only are candelabra as such symbolic: their very design may add a further layer of meaningful symbolism.

A very traditional take on candelabra is to shape them in the form of a tulip flower (laleh), such as the example pictured.

THE HOLY BOOK(S)

The Holy Book is typically the very first item purchased by the couple for the wedding table. It is there to signify and symbolize the couple asking God directly for His blessings upon them and their marriage. It also symbolizes the importance of prayer in the marriage. Like the mirror, it is one of the more serious elements of the Sofreh Aghd, and its meaning is intended to stay close to the couple forever in their marriage and life together.

During the wedding ceremony itself, the couple sits side-by-side and holds the Holy Book(s) in their laps as they agree to be married. Once the wedding has concluded, the Holy Book(s) go into the home of the couple. This is done so that the energy of the love and the blessings from God may always remain in their presence. These are wonderful and meaningful traditions, rich in symbolism and poetry; it is the presence of a Holy Book specifically that makes them possible.

If religious texts, for

whatever reason, are not to be used, Bijan Moridani thoughtfully suggests the Hafez Book of Poetry – "essentially the highest literary symbol of love in Persian culture," as he puts it. And if Holy Books from more than one tradition are to be used, that is not an issue at all: as a rule, multiple or variant heritages and Holy Books are entirely acceptable nowadays, and two can surely find a place in the overall theme of your Sofreh Aghd. Hebrew Scriptures may sit beside the Q'uran and both will be entirely welcomed and celebrated; a Christian New Testament and Buddhist scriptures can rest alongside one another with all the harmony of the couple that selected them. Indeed, they will serve as symbols of that harmony and of a longing for a universal harmony.

Just as God's universe is large enough to encompass many faiths and a universe of diverse perspectives, so the Sofreh Aghd, which in so many ways symbolizes the universe within and without, is large enough to encompass two Holy Books.

FLOWERS

Gol

The symbolism of flowers is infinite. In general they are on the Sofreh Aghd to add beauty. Even better, the flowers chosen can add additional meaning and symbolism to the Sofreh Aghd, depending on the background of the couple. To Westerners (and not only to Westerners) red roses traditionally indicate passionate love, and white roses are associated with innocence, virtue and purity. A lotus may be uniquely appropriate if either bride or groom is of Asian or Indian extraction – the Lotus is the national flower of India, and the Hindu deity Vishnu is often called the "Lotus-Eyed One," since the unfolding petals of the Lotus suggest the expansion of the soul. In Buddhist symbolism, the lotus represents purity of the body, mind and speech: according to legend, the infant Buddha was born with the ability to walk, and Lotus flowers would bloom everywhere the infant stepped.

While you are not absolutely bound to follow tradition, traditionally the floral arrangements are positioned in parallel on each side of the central mirror; and both sides should either match or harmonize beautifully together — like the wedding couple themselves.

Termeh: The Silk Cloth

The Termeh is a beautifully hand-woven silk or wool cloth which sits in the center of the Sofreh Aghd. It is nothing if not striking: the background colors generally used in a Termeh are jujube red, light red, green, orange and black.

The creation of Termehs is an ancient Persian art most famously associated with the city of Yazd in Iran. The Termeh is as old as Persia itself, is deeply revered and has long been celebrated: Greek historian Herodotus and Avesta writings celebrate Iranian gold and silk weave.

Termehs are generally passed down in families or purchased as a gift by family. Also, it carries religious connotations: the Termeh is often called, or used, as a prayer rug, and its presence on the Sofreh Aghd is intended to remind the couple of the importance of prayer to God. For this reason, among the devout, the Termeh may bear a small cube of clay with prayers written on it (Mohr) and rosary-like beads (Tasbih). Non-Muslim or more secular families may or may not include these, but the presence of a Termeh is a given.

HONEY AND YOGURT

Asal & Mast

Symbolically, sweet items in the Sofreh both describe the sweetness of the situation and the many wishes for a sweet life shared by the bride and groom. So it is simply mandatory to have a cup of honey on the wedding spread. Immediately after the couple is formally married, the bride and groom each dip one finger – the fifth, pinky finger – in the cup of honey and feed the honey to one another.

The symbolism of honey has roots in Persian culture that pre-date even the culture itself: The fertility god of Egypt, Min, was offered honey; in Islam, an entire Surah in the Q'uran is called al-Nahl ("The Honey Bee"). Indeed, according to hadith, the Prophet Muhammad (peace be upon him) strongly recommended honey for healing purposes.

What does Yoghurt symbolize? Good health. But it is not there just for symbolism, but because Iranians simply love it and serve it at almost every meal, whether plain over other foods, as yoghurt cheese, as dugh (a mix of yoghurt, salt, and mint mixed with water) or as part of the national meal, Chelo kebab (a mixture of yoghurt, rice, well-marinated meat, raw egg and the spice sumac).

ROCK CANDY

Nabaat

Rock candy is another symbol of life's sweetness and love's sweetness, and the rock-like crystalline look of this particular sweet sometimes is taken to express hopes for a particularly enduring sweetness.

Rock candy is an inviting item for creative Sofreh designers, for the candy itself lends itself to carving, leading to some quite innovative set pieces for the Sofreh Aghd. In some cases, the rock candy is not put in a bowl, because it *is* the bowl: this is called Shakh-e-Nabaat. Sometimes the term is used of other carven or designed rock candy items or even when small polished bits of rock candies are sprinkled like jewels over other items of the Sofreh.

Ladies, beware! Some people may come and quietly sneak a nabaat away from your Sofreh Aghd for their tea. It's said that if you drink your tea with nabaat from a Sofreh Aghd, your luck will increase greatly. Since luck is welcomed by everyone, a wise Sofreh designer keeps a wealth of nabaat on hand, for it's certain that guests needing an extra boost of luck or good wishes will slip away a piece to include with their tea at the reception.

BREAD, CHEESE, GREEN HERBS

Naan-o-Paneer-o-Sabzi

Naan-o-Paneer-o-Sabzi is a placement of bread, cheese (generally feta cheese) and herbs (or simply greens). Strict traditionalists limit the greenery to traditional Persian sabzi: parsley, cilantro, green onions, mint, and of course beautiful varieties of lettuce.

The trinity of bread, herbs and cheese convey multiple meanings; the white cheese is said to represent purity, and the items overall express the wish for good health for the couple. Naan-o-Paneer-o-Sabzi symbolizes basics, fundamentals, foundations. But principally Naan-o-Paneer-o-Sabzi symbolizes community.

Traditionally Naan-o-Paneer-o-Sabzi is served to the guests at the end of the ceremony. The intent is to express that happy times are shared. All those present want to share their happiness with the couple, and the couple wants to share their happiness as well. The sharing of the bread, cheese and herbs express this, and it's said to increase the luck and good health of the couple and all who wish them well. Like the rock candy, having the naan-o-paneer-o-sabzi is said to significantly increase your luck.

FRUIT

Miveh

There is always fruit on the Sofreh, and it is usually seasonal. Unique color and shape configurations are prized and unusual or rare fruits are welcome. However, some fruits are all but required, in particular, apples, grapes and especially pomegranates. All fruits represent good health, but the three above are sometimes termed "the heavenly fruits," prized and chosen for their spiritual significance.

The Prophet Muhammad, peace be upon him, is said to have remarked that one seed from every pomegranate comes from Paradise, and so we must be especially careful not to drop a single one. Apples are said to symbolize the divine creation of mankind, and of course, go back to the Garden of Eden narrative shared by Christian, Muslim, and Jewish alike. And grapes contain the promise of wine, and wine is an echo of the Eucharist and God's love in the Christian tradition and a universal symbol of life's blood.

Fruits, apparently simple to prepare, may seem a less complex element of the Sofreh. Not so: the fruit is often ingeniously cut, arranged or designed and laid out with beauty and brilliance.

"CONGRATULATIONS" FLATBREAD

Naan-e Sangak

Of course there must be a place on the Sofreh Aghd to wish the couple warm congratulations on their marriage. The word for "Congratulations" in Farsi is "Mobarak Baad," and it is common to write Mobarak Baad in calligraphy on a specially baked and decorated flatbread dedicated for that purpose. The writing is usually written using either saffron ("Zaffaron"), cinnamon or Nigella seeds.

The Naan-e Sangak is not generally eaten at the wedding; a separate platter of this flat bread, feta cheese and fresh herbs – the aforementioned Naan-o-Paneer-o-Sabzi – is there to be shared with the guests after the ceremony.

Also, there is no reason to restrict congratulations to that item alone. Mobarak Baad can be written on a variety of items, food or otherwise, as a creative touch to your own wedding table.

The bread symbolizes prosperity and good health – the bread of life.

A Tray of Seven Spices

Khoncheh

A properly done Sofreh invariably has a stand-alone tray of Seven Spices, arranged in seven distinct colors and placed on the wedding table. The spices protect the couple from the "Evil Eye" (the bad intentions of others who do not wish them well). They guard them from and drive away evil spirits and bad feelings generally. (They also taste good.)

These seven spices are: Khashkhash (poppy seeds), Berenj (wild rice), salt, Raziyane (Nigella seeds aka coriander or fennel), Cha'i (black tea leaves), Sabzi Khoshk (Angelica) and Kondor (Frankincense).

Salt and tea leaves, wild rice and poppy seeds, you know. But you should also know that seeds of the Persian spice Golpar, which grows wild in Iran, are often mislabeled as Angelica. Accept no substitutes. Golpar is certainly welcome at the table, but not if you want to drive away demons. Go with Angelica. 'Nigella' is sold in the United States as coriander or fennel. And while frankincense is most often used in perfumes and as incense, it's easily commercially available. (And tasty.)

Seven Colors of Espand

Espand (wild rue) performs a very important part of the wedding ceremony – the warding off of "bad vibes" or bad energy generally. Espand seeds are thrown over burning coals, and the smoke which arises from the coals neutralizes any negativity around the couple which anyone wishing them unwell may have projected into their space. As the espand seeds hit the coals, you can hear them pop; the more popping, the more "bad energy" is neutralized!

In more traditional services, a brazier called a Manghal contains the burning coals sprinkled with the wild rue, a popular Iranian incense. But it is acceptable nowadays to burn espand as you would burn other incense, in a special bowl or holder. Used in many Zoroastrian ceremonies, rituals and purification rites, espand was (and is) believed not only to cast away mental and spiritual negativity, but also to foster vitality and health.

Espand is burned for the couple before the wedding ceremony. Of course, the purpose of having additional espand on the Sofreh is to bring even more protective energy to the couple, to the event and to the guests as a whole.

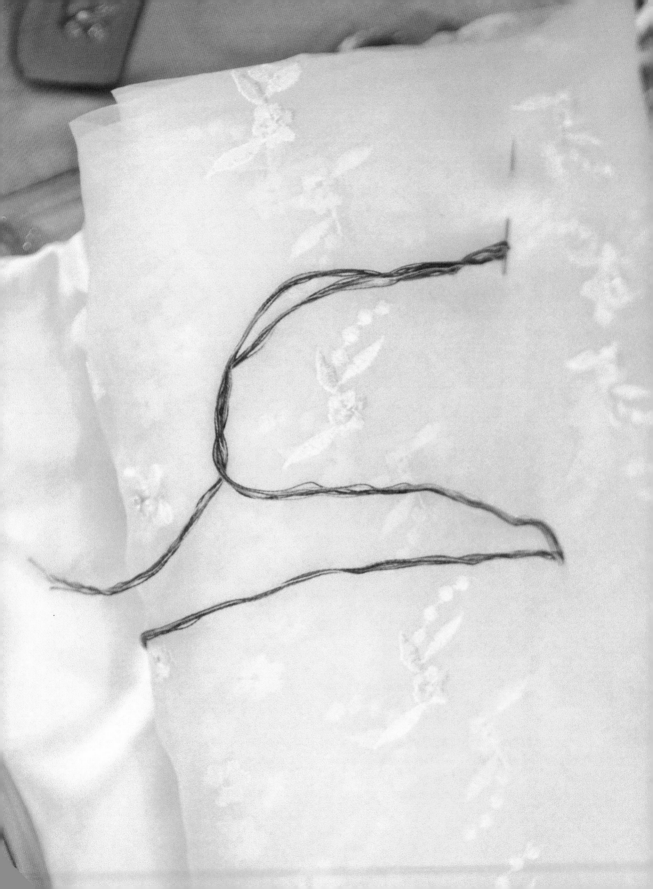

SEVEN COLORED THREADS (AND A NEEDLE)

Soozan-o-nakh

A Sofreh Aghd always includes a needle with seven different colors of thread on it. Why? One story has it that traditionally a Persian bride would be taken to a bathhouse on the day of the wedding. The women of family of the bride and the groom would gather there, wash the bride, clean her, feed her sweets and hold the veil used in the wedding ceremony over her head. One of the women would sew a needle with seven bright colors of thread on it through the veil over her head, for good luck.

But it may also be that well-wishers are seeking yet one more way to include further colors and again the number 7, traditionally considered auspicious and one that has already appeared in the form of seven spices.

GOLD COINS

Sekkeh Talla

An abundance of gold coins symbolizes wealth and prosperity for the wedding couple – in fact, an abundance of gold coins *is* wealth and prosperity, for the couple and anyone else! While cash amounts will be put into the hands of the couple, as well as collected throughout the wedding reception, these gold coins are special – and paradoxical. They are a symbolic wish for the couple to have more than enough money all the time. But they themselves will never be spent.

Once the ceremony is over, the gold coins on the Sofreh will be placed in a small pouch and sewn shut – forever. They will remain in the couple's home unspent – but radiating prosperity and energetic, ever-growing abundance, blessing the couple.

It is said that while gold coins represent wealth, to refrain from ever using them both symbolizes and demonstrates the freedom of the couple from the demons of greed and materialism, a freedom from those spiritual weaknesses and forms of want that no prosperity can ever fulfill.

Rosewater

Gol-ab

Rosewater is widely used throughout the Middle East to add a distinctive fragrance to foods, as a perfume, and to scent a space. So here; its role is to sweeten the air and bring a lovely fragrance to the entire Sofreh Aghd.

But its distinct scent is paralleled by a distinct taste used heavily in Iranian cuisine and especially in sweets such as nougat (gaz), raahat and baklava. Rose water is also used to give gulab jamums, and some varieties of loukum (sometimes known as 'Turkish Delight') their unique flavors.

Of course, all things Persian are saturated in history and tradition; and rosewater is no exception. Food aside, rosewater also has a long history of use as a perfume utilized in Eastern Orthodox, Hindu, Zoroastrian and Muslim religious ceremonies – indeed, a mixture of Zamzam Water and rosewater is used to clean the Kaaba itself.

And the very creation of rosewater – made from rose oil, also called attar of roses, a mixture of essential oils obtained by steam-distilling the crushed petals of roses – was first developed in (where else?) Persia.

ALMONDS AND WALNUTS

Badam-o-gerdoo

Nuts – plain, salted, sweetened and decorated – are beloved by Iranians, and that love is by no means restricted to almonds and walnuts. Those two are traditionally present on the Sofreh, but it is a wise and gracious host that adds hazelnuts and pecans and nuts in abundance of every variety. Indeed nuts are a symbol of abundance and renewal, and represent health and nourishment for the body, plus the wish that there will always be healthy food in the home of the couple.

Is any nut better left off the table? Yes: the cheaper, store-bought varieties. It is highly unlikely that you will ever see salted peanuts or anything remotely resembling "junk food," however much otherwise indulged in on a Sofreh Aghd.

Nuts do not only convey financial or personal abundance. According to some interpretations, nuts also represent good wishes for the fertility for the couple and a hope for the blessing of children upon the marriage as well. A basket of unshelled nuts is the particular symbol of this wish.

SWEETS

Shirini

Sweets are everywhere during Persian dinners, Persian gatherings, and in particular during Persian weddings and wedding receptions. They are so much a part of Persian culture that not to have sweets on the Sofreh Aghd is simply unthinkable.

What do they symbolize? The goodness of, well, everything – the sweetness of love, of life, of friendship, of family, of celebration, or marriage, of the past and the future and the present and of everything good that has been or is to come. "Life," as the saying goes, "is sweet." And sweets are on hand everywhere to remind everyone of this at every moment. And also because they taste sweet!

The sweets on the Sofreh are typically shared among wedding guests at the conclusion of the ceremony. The guests accept them because anyone with taste buds would be silly not to, but also because, traditionally, having one or more of these particular sweets phenomenally swells one's good luck.

Sweets are infinite in their variety, from candy to chocolate to nougat to mint. Baklava is shown here, although any sweet – beautifully arranged, of course – is acceptable for the wedding table.

NOGHL: A TRADITIONAL PERSIAN SWEET

While *all* sweets are welcome at the wedding table of a Persian wedding, some sweets are *particularly* welcome. Among these special sweets, the Noghl reigns supreme. No reception, or Sofreh, is complete without it. Noghls are to Iranians what hot dogs are to Americans. They simply cannot be overlooked. And including them is a given, especially once you taste a few.

What *is* a Noghl? Noghls are sugar-coated almonds especially prized by Iranians and Afghans. (You may have heard that the Afghan people call them "nuql" and toss them at Afghan brides and grooms like confetti. *Don't* confuse the two national traditions, however, and throw nuts at the Persian wedding couple.) Noghls are traditionally passed to the guests at the conclusion of the ceremony, and generally served with tea. These delicacies are made by roasting almonds, and then coating them in a solution made by boiling water, sugar, and rosewater together. Noghls aren't restricted to almonds: walnuts and pecans and other nuts are fine too. This particular snack is said to have been commonly used in ancient Persian wedding ceremonies, so its continued use in modern-day Persian weddings comes as no surprise.

EGGS

Tokhm-e-morgh

Eggs, of course, represent fertility and are placed on the Sofreh to express hopes for a fruitful marriage, strong and healthy children and indeed for a long and honorable lineage.

The key design element here is not arrangement so much as direct decoration. (Think Easter Eggs with a decidedly psychedelic turn.)

The decorated eggs on a Sofreh are sometimes among its highest art and each egg decoration may be a case of pure design, historical patterns, insignia or calligraphy, or shine forth its own unique symbolic display, carrying images of everything most dear to the couple.

Two Sugar Loafs

Kalleh Ghand

Kalleh Ghand are sugar loafs. We met them earlier, during ritual bathing ceremonies, where sugar loafs were rubbed over the head of the bride to presumably make her even sweeter, if possible, than she would normally be.

That ritual appears to have been retired, but it has a successor. Nowadays, during the wedding ceremony, the bride and groom sit in front of the Sofreh Aghd and a veil is held over their heads. One by one the happily married female members of the bride's family and the groom's come up and rub the sugar loafs together over the bride and groom's heads, sprinkling a snowfall of sweetness onto the veil and, by implication, over the couple.

It's said that this allows women in the families who are already happily married or are happy in life, to come and share their good energy with the bride and groom, so they too can join them in happiness. Unhappily married or divorced women may refrain from rubbing the sugar loafs for this reason; but it certainly should not preclude women who were unhappily married and are now happily single, and full of good wishes for the couple.

THE CLOTH HELD OVER THE COUPLE

During the wedding ceremony, a sheer fabric is held over the heads of the wedding couple. One by one the happily married female members of the bride's family and the groom's family come up and rub sugar loafs together over the bride and groom's heads. The sugar falling onto the cloth symbolizes a sprinkling of sweetness falling onto the couple and their future together.

Before and after the sugar loaf ceremony, the fabric, the threads and the needle are given a place of honor on the Sofreh.

THE TABLE CLOTH

The items of the Sofreh Aghd are not restricted to the items *on* the Sofreh Aghd. No less important are the chairs in which the couple sit at the Sofreh Aghd, and the table cloth on which items will be placed. The table cloth is traditionally white, which symbolizes purity, but otherwise may vary from a simplicity and plainness intended to highlight the other items, to an intricately sewn material or heirloom intended to proclaim the quality of the family and the union.

THE CHAIRS FOR THE COUPLE

Sandely

The wedding couple has seats especially assigned to them at the Sofreh Aghd. These seats are called the Sandely. Symbolically, it is not too much to consider them thrones. This tradition stems from ancient days – like the Japanese, ancient Persians often seated themselves on or near the floor, and so the traditional Wedding Spread table is not placed at waist height, like most Western dining tables, but is placed either on the floor or very near it. Since the Wedding Spread table is often only a few inches above the ground, it follows that seats generally are too.

In the spirit of all else at a Persian wedding, the chairs are specially decorated for the couple and often reflect their personal tastes of individual traditions.

OPTIONAL CONSIDERATIONS

The items mentioned so far in this chapter are more or less mandatory. You can have a Persian wedding without them; but if you do skip them, Persians will not think of it as such. The good news is that you can be extraordinarily flexible with them; you can indulge your creativity and your imagination to the farthest degree, and you will be applauded. But there's even more good news: you aren't restricted to traditional items. You can add almost anything you want that fits your theme – and who you are.

COMMON ADDITIONAL ITEMS

1. Henna: If you don't host a formal Hana-Bandan party (see the Hana-Bandan chapter), you can place henna on the wedding table for good luck. Or even place some henna on one another there, just as you would at the usual ceremony.

2. Butterflies (or Doves!): Butterflies and even doves can be released at the end of the ceremony for good luck – and to provide one of the most beautiful and memorable touches any wedding can have.

3. A Fancy Tray: An exquisitely and elaborately decorated tray for holding the rings – what could be more appropriate or impressive or lovely?

4. *Elegant Pouches For Gifts:* Gifts will be collected for the couple throughout the events. But in what? Surely not plastic bags, or paper – that would be unthinkable. A bag will need to be placed on or near the Sofreh Aghd to collect gifts given to the bride and groom after the ceremony. Why not make them beautiful and beautiful in ways that reflect your Sofreh's theme?

5. *An Elegant Pen:* It is certain that you will keep the pen with which you sign your marriage contract all your days. Does it not go without saying that it should be as beautiful, as touching, as evocative and precious, as that moment itself? The pen with which you write should be exactly like the spouse beside you: select the best.

Those are only a few ideas – I'm sure you will be able to come up with more.

And that is the key thing to remember.

The Sofreh Aghd is *not* formulaic and constrained: it is rich and living! The Persian wedding is a party! Yes, people go there in large part to wish a fine couple well and to cheer them on – but also to be surprised and entertained and impressed and startled! A Sofreh Aghd that is done completely by the book is a failed Sofreh; for it does not express the individuality, the uniqueness and the joy and life of the couple of which it is the supreme expression.

So while the elements you've seen so far are, I think, a good outline of all the absolutely necessary elements required by a Sofreh Aghd, filling in that outline – filling it with color, splendor and individual creativity – is what a truly splendid and memorable Sofreh Aghd is all bout.

And making it truly splendid is up to you

PREPARING YOUR SOFREH AGHD

1. Choose the size of the Sofreh Aghd first

You don't want any empty areas, so if you're going to have a large Sofreh Aghd, make sure your items are large enough to fit on it properly.

Once you decide how large you want your Sofreh Aghd to be, you will also need to figure out how large the base fabric covering of the table should be for the spread.

(Our Sofreh Aghd as shown in this book was 7 feet by 6 feet.)

2. Choose the base fabric for the Sofreh

The base fabric should be a beautiful high-quality fabric. It does not absolutely have to be white, but generally it is.

3. Choose a color theme for the Sofreh

Have an overall color scheme in mind. I wanted gold and crystal. A color scheme will help dictate the style and design of other items you purchase for the Sofreh Aghd.

4. Choose an overall design

Do you want your Sofreh Aghd items to lie flat or do you want them on stands? Or would you prefer to see them layered in tiers on boxes? Do you want perfectly symmetrical placement or something looser and more organic? Decide beforehand.

5. Decide on your preferred general style (simple, stylish, lavish, crystal-themed, etcetera)

The possibilities for designing a Sofreh Aghd are truly endless. Like snowflakes, no two are ever alike. But once you decide on a general style, your subsequent style and design decisions will be much easier to make. For instance, there will be eggs on the wedding table to symbolize fertility. If your stylistic preference emphasizes crystal, then you may seek out beautifully colored crystal eggs to place in your Sofreh Aghd design. If your theme is lavish, you may choose to find large beautifully embellished and meticulously hand-painted eggs with Persian design themes.

The possibilities are infinite – so, you need to focus them by arriving at a clear idea of your own most strongly desired stylistic preferences. Choosing the style you hold most dear for your Sofreh, will help guide you to make your perfect Sofreh an unforgettable reality.

6. Get the basics, take it easy and take things step by step

The Sofreh Aghd can seem overwhelming. It doesn't have to be. Concentrate on the basics first, choose the items one by one and just make progress, little by little. If everything's not perfect, that's okay. It will be, just give it a little time. You can get very creative in the decorating stage, so long as you collect all the necessary items first.

7. Decorate and embellish the items according to your chosen theme

Did you imagine that all you need to do for your Sofreh Aghd is to buy something and place it on the wedding spread? Don't be silly! Why do you think glue guns and ribbons were created? You can have items that are not lavishly decorated, if simplicity is your theme; but if lavish decoration is your theme, go for it! Drape every egg with ribbons and spangles, and tie every sprig of herb with strings of gold! Be as creative as your imagination pleases.

IMPORTANT ADDITIONAL CONSIDERATIONS

1. Choose *before* the wedding whether or not you would like your Sofreh Aghd on a riser.

We used a three- inch riser which measured 7 feet by 6 feet. Risers are perfectly fine, just be sure that the place you plan to have your wedding has a riser available for use, or that you can rent one and have it available on time.

2. Ensure *before* the wedding that there are outlets available close by should you plan on using electric lamps or other devices.

If half the beauty of your sparkling crystal-themed Sofreh Aghd rests on the lamps beaming onto them, and there are no outlets to power the lamps, the whole effect will be lost. Check beforehand!

3. If you have an open flame on your candles, make certain your facility will allow them to be lit.

Make certain that there are no unexpected minor requirements that can spoil your carefully crafted effects.

For example? For example, many facilities require that you cover open flames by placing them in a holder which is at least three or four inches taller than the flame. If that means you have to toss away the holders you've searched for carefully for weeks and months, and that are possibly a treasured heirloom that must be in the ceremony, so it can be a disaster. Know the rules!

4. Assign two to three people *minimum* to set up the Sofreh.

5. Arrange for the transportation of the items to the ceremony site.

And don't forget that the items are delicate. Some may need to be hand-held or packaged very carefully.

THE PLACEMENT OF THE SOFREH AGHD

For very traditional brides, the room chosen for the wedding ceremony (which is the room containing the Sofreh Aghd as well) should be bright, and there should not be an empty room under the ceremonial room (an empty basement or garage, for example).

For our friends who are observant Muslims, the Sofreh is placed facing North-east towards Mecca.

For our friends who honor Zoroastrianism, it often follows Zoroastrian custom to place the Sofreh Aghd near a body of water, for good luck.

Hire A Designer or Prepare Your Own Sofreh Aghd?

As I've said, the Sofreh Aghd is the centerpiece of the Persian Wedding. Whether you choose to have a small or large wedding ceremony, the Sofreh Aghd will stand out as the quintessential element of your Persian wedding celebration. For this reason alone, it must be as beautiful and well-made as it is possible to make it.

As a bride making the preparations, you must therefore make a decision early on as to whether you would prefer to put your own Sofreh Aghd together with the help of your friends and family, or if you would prefer to hire a professional Sofreh Aghd designer to create your dream Sofreh Aghd.

Here's the good news: both options are great options. There are obvious benefits and pleasures to preparing the wedding table yourself, and there are equally obvious benefits to having a professional prepare it. I have gone through, and seen, the rewards of both approaches, and you won't go wrong choosing either. The only question is, do you have the time and resources to do it yourself? If so, you're sure to take great pride and enjoyment in your choice. If not, a professional can lift an immense amount of labor and concentration needed elsewhere off your shoulders.

Just know that you can do it without calling in a professional. We did ours alone, and the result was spectacular. However I was lucky: I had a mother-in-law with an abundance of time on her hands, creativity in her heart and knowledge of, and experience with the Sofreh Aghd. I was blessed.   I   would love to take full credit for the marvelous Sofreh Aghd she prepared, but she was the star who handled it from start to dazzling finish. I have all the items in my Sofreh Aghd on display at my home, and I will always remember and cherish the loving energy she put into preparing our wedding table.

But you may not have anyone as gifted, experienced or seasoned, or with enough time available to undertake the many subtle tasks associated with designing such a Sofreh Aghd. That's fine – there's absolutely nothing wrong with hiring an expert to help you design your table. Brides are no more required to create their own Sofreh Aghds than they are to sew their wedding dresses by hand or smelt their own rings on a forge.

But the key point to remember is that you must make your decision early in the process. The Sofreh Aghd is not something you can throw together at the last minute.

It must be remembered that the Sofreh Aghd is not at all a mere collection of required items, but an expressive statement. While the items on the sofreh may be formally the same, the design, color, decoration and overall creative impact of each element are completely individual and completely different from one Sofreh Aghd to another.

In fact, the Sofreh Aghd is primarily an expression of the personality, taste and artistic ability of whoever is designing it. Does that mean that only the couple or their immediate family can create one? No. But a hired professional must be like an accomplished portrait painter: he or she must be able to catch the essence of the couple's style, their essence and their poetry and transmute it into the quintessential expression of their mutual love that is the Sofreh Aghd. For that reason, the person who designs your Sofreh Aghd will play quite a special role in your wedding.

WHAT YOU MUST HAVE TO PREPARE YOUR OWN SOFREH AGHD

Traditionally, the preparation of the Sofreh Aghd is a family event. It is especially so for the mothers and daughters and other women in the families of the bride and groom. Every Persian mother dreams of the day she can prepare her daughter's Sofreh Aghd.

Given the emphasis on family and friends in

traditional Iranian culture, it's not an overstatement to say that every Persian woman too, at some point in her life, contributes to a friend's or family member's Sofreh Aghd. So it is all but inevitable that close female friends will readily and eagerly participate in its creation, if asked to do so. Yet they may not be, and that is acceptable too. Many a Sofreh Aghd design will be shrouded in secrecy till the unveiling, since many a couple and their designer will not want to give away any of the creative and surprise elements they plan to incorporate. The goal in both cases is the same: every Persian bride wants her Sofreh Aghd to shine brighter than the sun. For this reason, many people choose take great efforts to make it perfect. One can reach for such a goal with the help of family or friends or with the help of a professional designer.

But if you are going without professional assistance, having the support and input of family and friends is key. If you want to reach your goal without professional support, you will need an abundance of the following:

TIME

How long will preparation take? At least six months to a year. The items need to be collected, decorated and embellished; some items may need to be brought in from Iran or specially made. Shopping for and finding the perfect items one by one may take time and organizing them after you find them may take even longer. This preparation is time-intensive. Be prepared for it.

MOTIVATED SUPPORTERS

If you and your fiancée are alone in the city where you are being married or if you only have a few friends willing and able to help you, think hard before taking this task on alone. You will have many other obligations needing your attention all at the same time – guest lists, invitations, mailing, the collecting of addresses, meetings with chefs, choices of linen, catering and cake design and many other ceremonial responsibilities.

If doing it all completely alone means taking on far more than you can handle, face it honestly. Find professional help.

If, on the other hand, you're living in a city with family and friends close by and family and friends who are highly motivated to help, it will be much easier to take on the task without hired assistance.

Be honest with yourself about your situation. An acquaintance may wish you well in all sincerity but not be able to commit a great deal of time to your

Sofreh Aghd; while a mother close by may be determined to see that you have the most spectacular Sofreh Aghd the world has ever seen. That is the kind of motivated supporter you need helping you!

Also, you will need people committed to certain special designated tasks – for instance, people who are willing to come early the day of the wedding and spend two to four hours setting up the Sofreh Aghd. You as the bride won't be doing that. You'll be far too busy getting ready and sipping champagne.

CREATIVITY

Let's face it: some of us are just not that artistically inclined. And even those of us who are don't necessarily excel at everything. Being able to take a good photograph doesn't mean you select an appropriate floral arrangement.

A certain degree of discernment applies to your choice of helpers too. Simply because you love your sister doesn't mean her sense of color harmony is unparalleled. Nor does it have to be. If neither you nor your closest friends are flowing with creative juices or particularly enthusiastic about the idea of creating a unique and original and beautiful Sofreh Aghd, that's fine. Just bear in mind that this is not the time to start.

A great Sofreh Aghd simply must have a solid overall sense of design and only highly creative minds can make the Sofreh Aghd truly shine. A dazzling custom-made Sofreh Aghd is the result of gifted, creative, passionately committed people who know how to make twenty-four different items flow seamlessly together and in perfect harmony. While designing or decorating item #17, you must always and at the same time be thinking of the overall finished vision as well as how your work harmonizes with items one through sixteen, as well as the rest that are to follow.

It takes a special kind of concentration, as well as unique gifts and enough time and space to exercise them to their highest degree. If you and your friends can do it, great! If not, that's fine too. There are plenty of people available who can create a Sofreh Aghd for you that you will never forget. Just know what your capabilities are and what you are getting into.

CHRISTEN'S TOP 5 REASONS TO PREPARE THE SOFREH AGHD YOURSELF

Does creating a Sofreh Aghd sound hard? Well – it is work. But it's exceptionally rewarding work, with many, many pluses.

For instance:

1. It's A Great Way To Bond

If you're new to Persian culture, there's probably no better way to bond with the Iranian side of the family. Making the Sofreh Aghd with Iranian family members is not only a fun and exciting way to expose yourself to Persian customs, language and traditions, in general, you'll constantly hear personal stories and remembrances as you work on items together.

Working on a Sofreh Aghd can sometimes feel like reviewing an entire family history in microcosm, and as someone taking part, you become a part of that history as well. There are few if any better ways to feel part of a wonderful family.

2. It's Not That Hard To Make

What? After all that I said about the high art and symbolic subtlety?

Well…think of it as being like cooking. Is it easy to create a dinner that will make the finest chefs of Paris burn with envy? No.

Is it easy to create a delicious, tasty, nutritious meal that family and friends will love? Actually, yes! (At least, if you know a little bit about it — and you do, if you're reading this book.)

The most difficult part of making a Sofreh Aghd

is figuring out what needs to go on the Sofreh and where it should go. This book has already done the research for you there; you can simply buy what's on the list and follow the diagram to see where to place the items. You can even search the internet nowadays and find a wealth of fine examples of model Sofreh Aghds to inspire you.

Remember, you can let your creativity flow when it comes to selecting specific items on the list. There must be a mirror, but you can make it as ornate or sleek, as gilded or as tinted, as you wish. There must be floral arrangements, but the possible combinations of flowers, scents and colors are infinite!

A Sofreh Aghd may be large, lavish and elaborate, but it doesn't have to be; indeed, some of the most beautiful and best-remembered Sofreh Aghds are simple, sincere and tastefully done.

Every Sofreh Aghd is stunning so long as it is made with love. And every time a Sofreh Aghd is prepared with love, the process is a joyous one.

How to do it? Start early and keep building it up and adding more and more creative touches. By the time the actual ceremony comes, your Sofreh Aghd will be dazzling.

3. YOU CAN LET YOUR PERSONALITY SHINE THROUGH

The point of your Sofreh Aghd is that it is yours and yours alone. A good designer can capture that individuality, just as a good portrait painter can catch the essence of a person. But who knows you better than you yourself? The Sofreh Aghd should reflect your taste in flowers, in fruit, in arrangement and in style. It should express who you and your spouse are as a couple and a family. If the bride is Iranian and the groom is not, or vice versa, integrate one another's separate Holy Books or combine flowers from both home countries. There are endless ways to incorporate the values and traditions of both the bride and groom into your Sofreh Aghd!

4. IT CAN BE DONE INEXPENSIVELY

In the United States, say the word "wedding" and the price of virtually any item seems to jump ten- to twenty-fold. Anything white, or traditionally associated with American weddings, is marked up – sometimes into the stratosphere. You may be under the impression that preparing something as unique as the Sofreh Aghd will be costly, but if you happen to be planning your wedding in the United States or anywhere outside Iran, you may have a distinct advantage.

You see, for the most part, no one knows that the Sofreh Aghd items are for "weddings," so you can often get a remarkably good price for each item. How expensive are fruit, spices or small decorative eggs after all?

Yes, a Sofreh Aghd can get very pricey and those involved can spend a great deal of money for high-end items (expensive crystal eggs, for example). But it doesn't have to be expensive. Expense alone is never the mark of a truly great Sofreh Aghd, any more than the greatness of a painting is judged by the cost of the paint. The true price of making a Sofreh Aghd is paid in time and love; the true value of a Sofreh Aghd is the love that it expresses.

Simple or lavish, the choice is yours. But expense as such is not the issue. Either way you can have a creatively designed, beautifully assembled Sofreh Aghd that says all that can be said to everyone's complete joy.

5. YOU KEEP THE ITEMS

In some wedding services, the items are traditionally taken back by the service providers and become part of their inventory for future use. Not so with the Sofreh Aghd. Each expense becomes an enduring asset. Each treasure becomes yours to treasure forever or pass on to your children and circulate within your family.

HIRING A PROFESSIONAL TO DESIGN YOUR SOFREH AGHD

If there are sound reasons to keep the design of one's Sofreh Aghd in the family, there are equally good and sound reasons to hire a professional to design your Sofreh Aghd.

As I've said, preparing the Sofreh Aghd is time-intensive and creativity is mandatory. The entire Persian wedding will in many respects be judged on the Sofreh Aghd. It is what people will most remember and as the very symbolic embodiment of the marriage, the love inspiring it and the universal good wishes for the bride and groom.

But there is no room for error. It need not be expensive. It need not be absolutely perfect. But it *cannot* be shoddy, neglected, thoughtlessly produced or something put together at the last minute. It must be good.

If you're busy or not terribly into the arts, don't attempt to do a Sofreh Aghd unless you're certain you can carry it through well. If you're at all uncertain, don't hesitate: call in a professional.

Also, if you are bound and determined to create a Sofreh Aghd that people will talk about for years, if you care nothing about the expense, if you want it to go completely 100% over the top, again – hire a professional! Save yourself the time, grief and stress of striving for absolute perfection on your own. Let the experts come in and do what they do all the time and what they do so very well.

What can you expect it to cost?

A Sofreh Designer will probably cost you, at the very least, around $2,000-4,000 to design the Sofreh, bring in the items, set them up and take them away. Travel expenses for the designer are an additional expense, and if you are looking for top of the line Sofreh design, your cost could soar exponentially upwards.

The decision is yours. However, considering what you receive in return, I think using a few thousand dollars of your wedding budget in this way is a very good way to use it.

What follows are my top five reasons for hiring a Sofreh Designer; and as you can see, they include the fact that the designer brings value to the wedding in many many more ways than just preparing the wedding table.

Christen's Top 5 Reasons To Hire A Designer To Make Your Sofreh

1. Stress Removal

A Sofreh designer will lift tons of stress from your shoulders, particularly if you're unfamiliar with Persian weddings, don't live near the Iranian members of the family, are a non-Iranian marrying "into" Persian culture or just plain have a million other things to do.

Even with lots of guidance, designing a Sofreh Aghd can be daunting and intimidating, and it is the centerpiece of the wedding by which the wedding as a whole will be judged. A Sofreh designer takes away all this stress and uncertainty and allows you to focus on other parts of the wedding.

2. Expertise

This is all they do. They are the experts. The specialists. The masters. The designers who run Sofreh designing businesses either have or hire the creative expertise needed to understand how the Sofreh Aghd is done to perfection. New and modern interpretations or classic traditional, these are the people who go to all the big Persian weddings, see all the simple and lavish Sofrehs and live, breathe and dream Sofreh Aghds. They can give you a thousand ideas since they spend all their time attending, assessing and reviewing Persian weddings.

If you do the same thing every day throughout your career, in time you become very good at your craft. These people are the best. They've seen it all, and they know what they're doing.

3. The Price Is Reasonable

Good Sofreh designers can be found for as little as $3,000 or so plus travel expenses. The prices can go all the way into the $100,000+ range for very experienced designers and if truly high-end items are planned for the Sofreh Aghd.

Of course, the Sofreh Aghd is not about money: it's about love. But the Sofreh designer isn't being asked to provide love – love is already there. He or she is there to help provide a design expressive of that love. But while money isn't the central issue, if you have the money, why not just go for it and make it as lavish and fabulous as you can! An inexpensive yet beautiful Sofreh Aghd is possible, and an expensive and beautiful one is possible too. It's all up to you and what you want.

4. The Sofreh Designer Knows It All

Sofreh designers know a heck of a lot more than just Sofreh design. They know all about every last aspect of Persian weddings. If you're unfamiliar with Persian weddings, trust me, it is not a bad idea at all to have someone available to answer a quick question about how this part of the ceremony or reception is carried out or how that dish should be served.

Sofreh designers do nothing but go to Persian weddings. This makes them as invaluable to you as a consultant as they are as designers. This resource alone makes them worth the money in time saved and headaches avoided! And speaking of time…

5. A Sofreh Designer Saves You Time

Come the day of the actual ceremony, you will likely be overwhelmed. There will be a hundred things to do. Your time then will be invaluable. Not to mention, you're getting married which is such a supremely exciting and emotionally enticing moment all on its own. It's a lot to process on top of hosting hundreds of guests for a lavish party. A professional Sofreh designing service can save you a huge amount of time simply by setting up the Sofreh Aghd and taking it down for you.

In the traditional Persian weddings of old, the Sofreh items were carried into the home of the bride by a caravan of family members. Yes, a caravan! Can you imagine that? I find that doubly amazing because of the care needed to deliver the items. Some of the items are nothing if not delicate when finished, and it takes a great deal of care to pack them into a car. You have to drive slowly as to not break or otherwise injure an item. The crystal chandeliers used to illuminate my own Sofreh Aghd were so delicate and elaborate that they had to be carefully and elaborately packed into boxes in multiple layers of wrapping and personally held while being transported. Trust me when I say the people at the wedding venue will be nervous even to store the items once they see how beautiful and delicate they often are.

This careful, delicate, sensitive work takes time. As the bride or groom, you must ask yourself who will have the time to do all this – and not just convey the Sofreh Aghd, but assemble it quickly, perfectly and properly. At my own wedding, we all arrived late to hair and make-up because the Sofreh Aghd took all morning – over five hours! – to properly set up.

We could have used five extra hours that day. I'm sure you'd benefit from five extra hours on your wedding day too. A Sofreh designer can give you that – and more. A Sofreh designer has seen and done what needs doing perfectly, hundreds of time. They know they have only one job on the wedding day: to make the centerpiece of the wedding perfect.

They will come prepared for everything. They will bring extension cords, extra glue, ribbons and additional items in case anything is broken or lost.

Most importantly, they have been working on your Sofreh Aghd and only your Sofreh Aghd, and they know precisely how you want it put together. So when it's finally your wedding day, you don't have to worry about it. At all. If you want, you can step away from the partying and the celebrations and peep in at the last minute for a spot-check and give everyone the OK.

What about all the rush, stress, worry, fear and labor you might have had to deal with? It never even appeared.

For this reason alone, hiring a Sofreh designer is a great *great* idea.

"It is love that holds everything together,
and it is the everything also."

— Jalal al-Din (Rumi)

Chapter 16:
Hiring the Perfect Vendors

A FEW NOTES TO GET YOU STARTED IN THE RIGHT DIRECTION

Ladies, haven't we all secretly wished we were living in Los Angeles when it's time for a good Persian wedding? Unfortunately, not all of us are so lucky. Most of us brides have to plan our Persian weddings outside of the Persian Mecca known as Los Angeles, where magnificent caterers, photographers, videographers and everything else wonderfully Persian abounds. It's a painful fact, but we must face it, if we want to make our dreams of having a fabulous

Persian Wedding come true!

So let's be honest and admit that, unless you do live in Los Angeles and have a multitude of Persian planners, caterers, Sofreh designers and so on at your  beck and call, you have two options. Either you will have to work with mostly American vendors who are used to working on American weddings and only American weddings or you need to bring in vendors experienced in working Persian Weddings from out of town.

It is of paramount importance to take this into consideration from the start: Your vendors will most likely not be familiar with Persian Weddings at all.

As you learn more and more about Persian weddings, you'll begin less and less to relate to the feeling of working on a project when you have little knowledge about the subject matter. In general for many vendors, the Persian wedding ceremony will be a complete unknown and that lack of knowledge can make your vendors nervous and uneasy about the event, as well as simply not knowledgeable. This is not a good situation. You want your vendors to be calm, comfortable, informed and creative. Help them get there if they aren't there yet. They may nod their head "yes" in understanding, but I assure you, you will be disappointed to realize how much they miss if you're not careful. I've heard this time and again from brides working with vendors unfamiliar with Persian ways, customs and the ceremonial structure in general. Make it your job to ensure they know the key parts of the ceremony and celebration to follow.

What can you do about it? Educate, educate, educate. And maintain calm. Your vendors want to do a good job, and they want you to be happy. You just have to clarify for them what it takes, and you have to stay alert to make sure they catch on properly.

WHO ARE YOUR KEY VENDORS?

Key vendors are the essential experts who will ultimately make or break your Persian wedding.

Because of their expert knowledge, they hold the key to making your Persian wedding exceptional and spectacular where it counts.

The Persian cuisine you serve, the Sofreh Aghd, the Iranian music – however small or large the event, these things must be exceptional. They must be truly Persian – not close fakes. More than anything, your key vendors will be vendors experienced in Persian weddings.

They will need no coaching or education about the ceremony. They will make things run smoothly where it counts. They are worth the money because they will make your life easy. Better to spend a little more for perfection, than a little less for a disaster or an embarrassment.

For this reason, I say: commit yourself to hiring one or two key vendors.

I had to go to Dallas and Chicago to bring in mine. But where you find them may surprise you. I found one of my key vendors, a chef, subtly disguised at a local country club. He had done his culinary training in California but knew how to prepare Persian cuisine flawlessly, all the way down to the metal skewers needed to make properly juicy Kabob.

What kinds of vendors are "key" vendors, you ask?

The Sofreh Aghd Designer
The Chef
The Photographer
The Videographer
The Wedding Planner

These assistants will make your wedding a dream come true. Let me share a few things with you: a few generalities to look for as you begin searching for the perfect team to create your very own Persian Wedding.

HIRE EXPERTS

If you have all the money in the world, then hire only people expert in servicing Persian weddings specifically. It's the only way to go if you can afford it. Even if you're on a budget like the rest of us, the cost of a hotel and plane ticket to bring in an expert is worth its weight in gold if it saves you twelve months of planning headaches. I was not in a situation where money was absolutely no object to me; therefore I mixed and matched. I hired the best when necessary and otherwise made the best of a non-ideal situation. I learned to make non-ideal situations work in my favor. You can too.

For instance, if you can't get a vendor with

at least some knowledge and experience in Persian wedding customs or can't afford one, fake it. By which I mean, look for vendors who have done Indian weddings. They may be open to an "exotic" or "different" type of wedding celebration.

Their enthusiasm or lack thereof will alert you to whether you should consider working with them.

ENTHUSIASM IS KING

If the vendors are unfamiliar with Persian Wedding customs, make sure that they want to learn more and are enthusiastic. An enthusiastic, excited vendor will bring loads of creativity and excitement to your Persian wedding!

High Priced Is Not Necessarily High Quality

For fairness sake, many of these vendors are able to charge such high prices because their reputation, service and products are phenomenal and they have earned their reputations by delivering to brides the creative and beautiful wedding of their dreams. However, with that said, even if a vendor is charging astronomical amounts of money to work your wedding doesn't mean they are the best fit for your event. Just be sure to read reviews on unbiased community websites and really evaluate their work and style before you sign anyone up for your team.

Look For Youth And Talent

Focus on finding creative, motivated and enthusiastic vendors. Young talent trying to break onto the wedding scene is a prime source of creative, motivated and enthusiastic service. They usually charge half of what more experienced vendors will charge, but they're 100% committed to getting your future referral, to building their name or brand and to showcasing their talent. They are hungry to make a living at their passion and you can take advantage of this by combining your enthusiasm with theirs. Not everyone new is excellent, but some are, and those are the ones to seek if you're on tight budget.

With enough self-education about what you need (such as this book) and a vendor who is eager and excited to do an exotic wedding, you can bring the vendor up to speed fast. Be encouraged: I was able to find and educate just such vendors. At the start they knew nothing whatsoever about Persian weddings and at the finish I had a wedding that was absolutely gorgeous.

I did it. You can too.

PERSIANS RULE

An inexperienced vendor with talent and a good attitude who is willing to learn is good.

A vendor with actual experience doing Persian weddings is better.

But even better than that is a vendor who's Iranian, period.

If they're Persian themselves or have otherwise been exposed to Iranian culture and customs regularly, they've attended Persian weddings by the score and all the fine details of the Persian wedding are second nature to them. Vendors like these are more than experts in their specialty: they're a precious informational resource. Don't educate them. Let them educate you!

With an experienced vendor like this, neither the bride nor the groom will need to give needed time for vendor education. Nor will an experienced vendor need to be micro-managed (something vendors dislike even when needed). If you can find someone like this, will it cost more? Pay it gratefully. Splurge on such hiring whenever you can. Trust me; it will be well worth the money.

But what if you live somewhere where Persian weddings are uncommon? Bring in your few crucial vendors from out of town. I planned my Persian wedding in the faraway

Persian kingdom of Tulsa, Oklahoma. Having an experienced vendor there was a dream! Not one single Persian wedding at all had been performed there for several years. My vendors had no idea what a Persian

wedding entailed. I thought it would take no time at all to get vendors unfamiliar with the details of the ceremony up to speed. I was wrong!

But I did make one very very smart move: I hired a few experienced key vendors. I went to nearby cities and paid for their transportation and hotel rooms if necessary. The cost was nothing compared to the level of expertise they brought to the event.

Chapter 17:
Jahaz-Boran

Unveiling of the Home Furnishings
and
A Wedding Shower

Introduction to the Jaheeziyeh

The Jaheeziyeh is Farsi for the home furnishings given to the couple from the family of the bride.

Jahaz-Boran is the wedding shower hosted by the bride's family. Like so many other event-stages in the Persian wedding process, the Jahaz-Boran is a party, a party as filled with music, laughter, dancing, joy and fun.

But at this particular party, the family of the bride will also show the couple items they've bought for the couple's new home.

The family of the bride will begin preparing for the Jaheeziyeh many years prior to the bride reaching a suitable age to marry. Really, it's not too much to say that for Iranian families Jaheeziyeh begins with the birth of a daughter. Just as in the United States, parents will begin saving money for college for their children the moment they learn that a child will be born.

For the Jaheeziyeh involves more than simply ensuring that the bride has a well-furnished and adequate home; though that, certainly, is its main object. The Jaheeziyeh is also a direct reflection of the family of the bride. The entire community will be watching and commenting. So no effort is spared to provide an impressive if not spectacular Jaheeziyeh. The sort of Jaheeziyeh the bride's family provides will define and confirm the stature a family holds in their particular community.

You may think that this means that the family

of the bride has to lavish the couple in ostentatious luxuries. Of course that isn't the case. Most people, Iranian or otherwise, are not extraordinarily wealthy, and marriage is certainly not restricted to the wealthy alone. No one expects families to go over their heads

into crushing debt purely to make a social splash. Indeed, families that spend obviously far more than their means are as likely to get a bad "review" as families that spend too little. As with all else in Persian wedding ceremonies, particularly those performed outside Iran, customization is the rule.

But… while there is certainly no requirement to supply objects of grotesque opulence, there is a clear pull toward providing several objects of quality and elegance, particularly such traditional items as elaborate and ornate Persian carpets, large luxury bedding, exquisite crystal chandeliers, specially designed pieces of furniture, high-quality china, statuary, wall hangings and paintings with traditional themes and so on. All are slowly purchased in advance, and all are thoughtfully and artfully purchased to reflect the family's image of itself and of its wishes for the bride.

This is an important point. Objects given in Jaheeziyeh are by no means a random assemblage of items bought on impulse and brought together piecemeal. They're not casual last-minute purchases from garage sales and eBay. As with the items of the Sofreh Aghd, Jaheeziyeh items are intended to represent the character of the family and the bride. Traditional families may focus or invest heavily in items with historical associations, such as tapestries or carpets. Trendier families may dazzle both the couple and the crowd with the latest and most massive HDTV.

The point is, the objects are not a haphazard collage of impulse purchases – the gifts are intended to say, "This is what our family is. This is the sort of home, the sort of lifestyle, appropriate to a daughter of this noble and admirable family." Needless to say, the tastes of the bride are considered too, as well as those of the groom. The furnishings are intended to furnish the couple's home after all. But the fact remains that the home furnishings are as much a public statement about the family as a whole as they are about the bride. And that statement itself is no small part of the gift. A couple that receives the gifts of a truly esteemed Jaheeziyeh are themselves held in deeper esteem.

ITEMS OF THE JAHEEZIYEH

What sort of gifts should the bride's family buy? Of course that depends on the tastes, resources and self-perception of the family. General rather than specific advice is the best guide. As I pointed out, expense as such is not as important a criterion as high – indeed sublime – quality. Typical larger items generally include living room furniture, major kitchen furnishings such as stoves and refrigerators, dining room sets and tables and bedroom furniture. Carpets and wall hangings – often the centerpiece in a Persian home – should also be placed here. A Persian family will never give anything but a magnificent carpet in Jaheeziyeh.

Art and what may be called decorative home items, such as lamps and vases, China and crystal, form the second tier. These can sometimes be quite elaborate and expensive, sometimes less so. In the third tier belong what might be termed more conventional shower gifts, though even these gifts are invariably top of the line in quality – gifts such as bedroom linens, towels, pillows, pots and pans, cutlery, kitchen utensils and cookbooks.

Finally there are items unique to Persian culture. Not everyone may think of them as household furnishings, but there is no Jaheeziyeh without them. Pajamas are one such item. Every Jaheeziyeh includes elegant sleeping clothing for the couple. One might expect chairs are always purchased, but in Persian culture some chairs are specifically designated for guests, and these furnishings are as a rule among the most finely designed and comfortable. A Jaheeziyeh that includes no items for showing courtesy to the couple's future household guests or for entertaining others is simply not a Jaheeziyeh.

RECIPROCITY OF LOVE IN PERSIAN WEDDINGS

If you've noticed a certain symmetry of generosity and a certain sharing of family responsibilities, you're not the first to do so. Generally, in Persian culture gifts are given and gifts are exchanged. Throughout the Persian wedding process, the family of the bride and the family of the groom will exchange gifts.

Is this a requirement? If the bride's family provides a magnificent chandelier, is the family of the groom expected to match it with an equally magnificent set of golf clubs? No, not at all. Such gestures come naturally from the heart and evolve naturally as the families interact.

The more you learn about the Persian wedding ceremony overall, the more you will come to appreciate its beautiful and natural, heartfelt, symmetry and balance. All concerned contribute; all concerned benefit; and all concerned are supported by a generous community of family and friends.

Weddings are expensive. Nowadays that is a given. But you would not be wrong to think of the Persian wedding as a set of acts of generosity which, in the long run, ultimately return value to the givers many-fold. The families who show such love and support for their children now will eventually be supported by their children, and those children will in turn will go on to support their children, who in turn will go on to love and support them.

It is not an out-of-pocket expense by a few individuals. It is the ongoing inheritance of a living and loving community.

This sense of equity goes far to explain why negotiation is so much a part of earlier parties, such as the Baleh-boran, during which the amount the bride's family will provide for the Jaheeziyeh is clarified. It's not merely that the Jaheeziyeh confers all the household items that the bride and groom will need in their new home. The amount of the Jaheeziyeh is traditionally balanced by the amount of the bride's dowry, the Mariyeh. If the groom's family is providing a high dowry, they can expect a similarly high Jaheeziyeh from the family of the bride.

There is balance. A balance springing from an unspoken but generous consensus of all parties involved as to what is just, loving and appropriate.

THE PRESENTATION OF THE JAHEEZIYEH

Sometime before the week of the wedding, the groom will have selected the couple's home, and the family of the groom will have arranged its purchase.

On the actual week of the wedding, women from the bride's family and from the groom's family will begin going to the home the groom has chosen and decorate it top to bottom with the furnishings that are part of the Jaheeziyeh.

It should be noted that the Jaheeziyeh is absolutely not simply a moving operation. Heavy items will already have been delivered by professionals. This part of the Jaheeziyeh is a decoration fest that turns – of course! – into yet another party event!

Like the Hana-Bandan, this part of the Jaheeziyeh is also one of the pre-marriage-ceremony parties which is unofficially restricted to a select group – in this case, female family members and close women friends only. Think of this part as being the closest equivalent of a bridal shower in American culture, except that those who attend will do so in the couple's actual new home-to-be.

This part of the Jahaz-Boran is quite informal. The bride's family brings the gifts of the Jaheeziyeh; the gifts are opened, praised and complimented. Then everyone discusses where to best place them in the home, which they then proceed to do. As a rule, the women make a wonderful time of decorating the home and setting everything up, and of course the bride is there directing it all, helping the women and arranging things so that everything is set up exactly the way she would like it.

Some aspects of this part of the Jahaz-Boran follow tradition. There should be sweets, tea, fruits and food available in the home to be offered during the party. Again, as with the Hana-Bandan, refreshments should be light. Espand will be burned for the bride-to-be to keep her protected from bad luck and from anyone so blind as to not wish her well.

One particular item in this part of the Jahaz-Boran should be remembered: a few small gifts should be purchased and wrapped beforehand for women from the groom's family and given to them when they all meet at the home.

ANCIENT PERSIAN JAHAZ-BORAN TRADITIONS

In ancient times the women would arrive not by foot but in a caravan, and they would enter the home bearing trays for the Jaheeziyeh, dancing to music, playing tambourines and burning the espand for the bride. Everyone in town would already know at once that a wedding was prepared, and the local women would also come in and peek to see what manner of Jaheeziyeh the bride was receiving. In the true tradition of Persian hospitality, the bride and her guests would invite the spectators to come in and be dazzled at the soon-to-be-bride's new home, join the party and spread the word about her joy and the generosity of her family throughout the community.

And, caravan aside, so it remains today.

*"The minute I heard my first love story,
I started looking for you,
not knowing how blind that was.
Lovers don't finally meet somewhere.
They're in each other all along."*

— *Jalal al-Din (Rumi)*

Chapter 18:
Band-Andazan

THREADING OF THE BRIDE

Days before the wedding the bride begins her beautification for the big day, and a party is held for her, called Band-Andazan.

This females-only gathering typically occurs two to three days before the actual wedding. Traditionally, Band-Andazan is the ceremonial "threading" (hair removal) of the bride's facial hair before the wedding.

At one time the event was quite a significant milestone in the life of a woman, since then it was unacceptable for women to remove any facial hair until they were married.

Things are different now; brides throughout the Band-Andazan will be beautifying themselves in far

more elaborate ways than removing an offending hair; the tone of this event is undeniably upbeat anticipation of the upcoming wedding.

The timing of this event is a few days before the wedding really to allow time for any unexpected redness or swelling from cosmetic preparations to dissipate before the wedding day.

While technically this event is to honor the bride, it is also a chance for her to relax with friends. The guests, limited to close female friends and family, not only help beautify their soon-to-be-wed family member and friend, but join with her in taking part in the lively music, dancing, tea sweets and fruits. They all joyfully celebrate and honor the bride in her final preparations for the wedding.

How, you ask?

While the bride is being prepared in a beautifully decorated chair, the female guests will merrily be dancing around her.

During the dancing, the guests will joyfully "daf" (play tambourines) which are beautifully decorated or the tar (traditional Persian instrument) around the bride as her face is being prepared.

As each guest passes her she will be handsomely shabashed (showered with money). The bride generally gives part of the shabash to the hired woman who is threading her face as a tip.

Then, the bride will join the celebration with her friends and family.

She will be one step closer to uniting with her beloved.

Chapter 19:
Hana-Bandan

THE PARTY THE NIGHT BEFORE THE WEDDING

HENNA PARTY!

Not all Westerners are as familiar with henna as are Persians and those of Persian ancestry. There, henna is widely known as a flowering plant used since distant antiquity to dye skin, hair and fingernails, as well as wool and leather. (Dye preparations derived from the plant and an art of temporary tattooing based on those dyes, are both also known as henna.)

The idea of "painting" henna on the bride and groom involves nothing so intricate or so permanent as tattooing.

But the use of the term "painting" is not entirely a metaphor: in ancient Persia, when women of that era painted their nails to enhance their

beauty, henna was the material of choice for that purpose. Brides then would even use it on their hair, to produce a deep rich color.

Nor was henna chosen for its attractive coloring alone – henna had long been considered a bringer of luck! The Persian social calendar has more than one occasion on which henna is used as a good luck blessing on persons or situations.

For instance, women may paint henna on their hands as a good luck ritual before Nowruz (the Persian New Year). The effect of the henna is not permanent, but it can take a long while to completely come off, and this is another symbolic reason for its inclusion in Persian wedding customs: it signifies enduring luck and lasting, ongoing happiness for the wedded couple.

The attractive look, the attraction of luck, the long traditional use, the signifying of a permanent joy – and, of course, the chance to throw yet another fabulous party – all this made it virtually inevitable that henna would be used at some point during Persian wedding ceremonies and indeed it has been given a ritual all its own: Hana-Bandan.

Hana-Bandan is both a party and a particular ritual that takes place in the course of the party. Like the ritual, the party has a certain looseness, but also certain characteristics unique to it that are generally observed. (I say "generally," because the Hana-Bandan, like every other element of a Persian wedding is there to celebrate the love of the bride and groom and the union of two families. It is meant to ensure a wonderful, memorable and happy time for all concerned.

Nothing could be further from the spirit of the Hana-Bandan or any element in a Persian wedding, than following rigid rules for their own sake.)

TIMING THE HANA-BANDAN

For example, the Hana-Bandan – the party and the ritual both – is traditionally supposed to be held the night before the wedding. But like every Persian wedding event, there is endless dancing, a wealth of food and sweets and drinks, ceremonies and bonding and camaraderie and music, and all of it is sure to run late into the evening.

All of it is quite enjoyable at the time, but a big party the night before the wedding can easily leave the bride and groom frazzled and tired on the big day. And what bride and groom want to find their heads nodding throughout the wedding ceremony?

For that reason, the Hana-Bandan is now held near, but commonly not immediately before, the day of the wedding.

LIGHT FOOD

One earlier facet of the Hana-Bandan may have come about precisely to address this. For in the Hana-Bandan, the dishes are often considerably lighter than in other parties. Tea, sweets, fruit and nuts are the cuisine of choice.

THE YOUNG AND THE HENNA

The light fare reflects another characteristic of the Hana-Bandan: it is uniquely a party for young people. Needless to say, all the elders in the family are invited, purely as a matter of politeness and respect. But as a rule the older people in the family and the younger all understand that this is a celebration for the young. Older family members send their good wishes for the event but politely excuse themselves "this one time." Because this one time it's understood that the party is for the young, and only young people are expected to congregate and to celebrate.

"Young" is an ambiguous term, however, and there's a certain delicacy involved in its application in the Hana-Bandan. A fifty-year old gentleman may consider himself in his prime, but he may not be considered in his prime by a thirty-year-old woman who regards herself as unquestionably quite young. And the woman herself may not be considered young not by the fourteen year-old who plans to bring along his new PlayStation games for the event.

How old is too old for Hana-Bandan? It's difficult to call, but fortunately for those who give the party, they're not required to call it. Everyone is invited, and everyone who is physically able to show up attends. Further, although this is traditionally a party for the "young" it is no longer so restrictive. All members of the family and friends who are close to the couple join in celebration and participate joyfully.

The "youth" and the lighter food are the special distinctions of the Hana-Bandan, but once the party actually begins, it functions much like every other Persian wedding party. The food (however light) is always plentiful, the dancing and music (which may lean toward suitably DJ'd techno) is vivid and continual, everyone is dressed to the hilt, chat and laughter are rich on all sides and everyone expects to have (and has) the time of their lives.

THE ACTUAL CEREMONY

There comes a point, though, when the ritual Hana-Bandan, the ceremony that is the traditional point of the party, must take place. The elders if close by will join the celebration for the ceremonial part. Especially the mothers of the bride and groom will be sure to join the party.

This is how that ceremony occurs:

The ritual is performed in the most beautifully

decorated room at the home of the bride. Two elegant chairs are set up for the bride and groom in a prominent spot so there can be no doubt that they are the center of attention. A fine table is set up not far from them, bearing ornate and exquisite bowls and dishes, colorful fresh flowers, and a tray bearing the ritual henna. The song Mobarak Baad ("Congratulations") song should be playing as the couple enter and take their places.

SHABASH: SHOWERS OF MONEY

Once the couple takes their places, one by one the party-goers approach them and... give them money.

Money? Not ornate statuary, gilded crystal or fabulous carpets?

No: tangible everyday currency, cash or money.

This may seem like a curious exception to the usual symbolism-rich character of Persian wedding gift-giving, but in fact it's yet another example of Iranian thoughtfulness. After all, the bride and groom are embarking on a new life together and starting a new family. Persians, raised in an old, wise and practical culture, know full well how very much money, plain and simple, can help a newly married couple. Those who love and care for the couple are expected to know that too and express their feelings financially. And they do.

To someone completely new to Persian custom, the effect can be a bit jarring. Sometimes the bride or groom's friend or family member will approach them and simply push cash directly into their palm! Some will be decorative about it and give them a semi-circular spread of money, like a Japanese fan. Still others will shabash (shower the money on top of their heads).

Both what is considered "money" and how people offer it is subject to a little variation. Sometimes money and a non-monetary gift are given for the bride and groom. There is nothing to stop the "money" from being the title to a property or a stock portfolio. Sometimes it need not be handed directly to the couple; on occasion a young girl may collect the money into a bag that's later given to the bride and groom.

HEART AND HAND

The mother (of the groom) will often be the one to officially begin the "money-giving" part of the ceremony.

Which hand receives the money is important: the mother of the groom will come up and stand somewhat behind the couple (throughout the process, the mother stands behind the bride and groom, so as not to block everyone's view) and to start off the money-giving, she will place money first in the left hand of the bride, and then secondly in the left hand of the groom.

The reason is that the heart is on the left side and since this is an occasion of the heart, the left hand must be used: since with the whole of their hearts they are promising to love one another. The left hand symbolizes this.

The mother of the bride comes up next, and she is the one that brings the henna tray. The mother of the groom then places the henna first on the left hand of the bride and then on the left hand of the groom.

(If either the bride or the groom prefer not to have their hands stained, it's entirely acceptable to place some money in the left palm prior to apply-ing the dab of henna and then dab the henna directly onto the money itself.)

In more traditional approaches, The henna is drawn specifically on the palm of the hand, not the backside, and the designs are traditional posi-tive Persian symbols – hearts, stars, the sun, and so on.

The couple then unites their left hands together

signifying their enduring love with an enduring mark of good luck. Some couples then wipe the henna off their hands immediately while others will leave it for extra luck.

Other Persian brides go further and have their nails stained with the henna for beauty and elaborate designs drawn on their hands for the wedding. Far from avoiding having their hands marked in this way, these couples welcome the process and the long amount of time needed for the henna to fade and come off because the semi-permanence of the henna conveys the promise that the couple will not only have good fortune, but lasting, enduring, permanent good fortune throughout their married lives.

SPICES, RICES, FLOWERS

After the henna has been placed and after the couple unites their designs hand to hand, then it is time to shabash the bride and groom. Shabash is the process of showering the couple in celebration with money, flowers, rice or spices.

Shabash is not necessarily restricted to currency. Espand (spices) are burned next, so that the scent may wash over the couple. After that, rice or flowers are thrown over the bride and groom. Finally partygoers themselves will come up and throw money over the heads of the couple or place it in their (left) hands.

SHARING THE SHABASH

Sometimes too, money circulates.

In one common tradition, money in the bride's hand is thrown at the single young men congregating at the end of the party. Whoever catches it or picks it up is the next to be married.

Then the money in the groom's hand follows suit. (Only in this case it's thrown to the young single girls).

A WISH COME TRUE

After the ceremony is over the tray of henna is carried around the room to the guests, who are invited to place the henna on their hands also. This is

a symbolic way for the couple to share with everyone
their joy and good luck.

It's also a symbolic way for everyone to join
into the happiness of the couple.

It's likely you will see many people whispering
a silent wish to themselves as the henna is placed on

Christen Flack Behzadi, M. D.

their hands. Why? Because very old tradition holds that any wish made when the henna of a Hana-Ban-dan touches one's hands is certain to come true.

Just as the deepest wish of the happy couple has come true. For tomorrow (or very soon) they are to be united as husband and wife at last.

Part Four:

THE PERSIAN WEDDING

Chapter 20:
The Legal Wedding

THE AGHD

THE TWO FACES OF THE PERSIAN WEDDING

At least two weddings generally take place. The legal wedding is first. The cultural Persian wedding, the one we've looked at up to now, is generally the second. These two weddings rarely take place on the same day. They may take place as much as a year apart from each other. Or even be all rolled up into one!

Culturally, the traditional Persian wedding ceremony (involving the Khastegari, Baleh-boran, the Sofreh Aghd, and so on) is regarded as the wedding. It is the public statement that the couple and families are joined. It is the event for public show, and it is deeply symbolic, profoundly meaningful and thoroughly social.

Nonetheless, the couple must legally seal their union as husband and wife, and the cultural Persian wedding does not do that, per say. Unless, of course, you take the necessary steps to have an appropriate officiate oversee the ceremony and add any additional statements necessary to legally seal the union.

You may wonder, why should the couple go through a cultural wedding at all, if a legal one is sufficient? The answer is that while a legal marriage is legally sufficient, it is not socially sufficient, at least not if you're Iranian.

The greater Iranian community is as much apart of these wedding unions between couples as the families are. Everyone takes an interest in a couple planning to be married, and the idea of just quietly eloping and letting that be all is almost unheard of in this sort of close-knit community.

THE LEGAL WEDDING

A legal wedding can be purely secular, but often is celebrated in the religious custom of the couple.

Meaning the first wedding can be anything from a courthouse ceremony with a judge, to a full-scale religious ceremony. This wedding too is called Aghd in Farsi. It is the legal Aghd.

As I pointed out earlier, the Persian wedding is a cultural ceremony; it is not considered a legal ceremony.[1] Thus, the legal Aghd is important in officially, legally sealing the union.

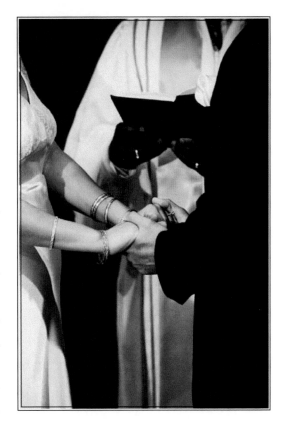

Now in terms of Persian marriage practices, imagine that an Iranian bride who is an Orthodox Christian wishes to marry an Iranian groom who is a Muslim. Imagine also that they met and live in Los Angeles, California. They will have a Persian wedding as so far described in this book because they are Iranian, and this is how Iranians do it!

[1] *That is, unless you choose to incorporate the appropriate legal steps with the proper officiant.*

But to have a legal union recognized by the United States government under which they presently live, they will have to follow up (or precede) their Persian wedding celebrations with a signing of American legal documents establishing their marriage legally in that nation. There may also be a ceremony in an Orthodox Christian church to seal the union in the eyes of that church for the bride and her family. There may be another ceremony in a mosque to seal the union in the eyes of Islam.

Legal ceremonies are generally far smaller and far faster. This ease may very well become a refreshing opportunity to slow down and enjoy a quiet, private time in front of 50 close family and friends instead of 500 at the main wedding. My husband and I had a separate small traditional American wedding with 35 guests in Muskogee, Oklahoma out in the country. It was so peaceful and beautiful to have a simple affair in front of our closest friends and family. There was no fanfare, and my family cooked up the feast. There were no wedding planners or elaborate décor needed. It was two people in love uniting in front of God, friends and family. It's wonderful to experience both the massive wedding affair and also the quiet family only ceremony as well.

Although its nice to slow down and have a small ceremony there are actual historical reasons traditionally why there are two separate weddings which we will briefly explore.

SEPARATION OF THE LEGAL WEDDING

It may seem strange that this "popular" public wedding isn't legal too, but there are some historical reasons for this, which we'll shortly touch on. The most important of those reasons is that in the Middle East, men and women for a long time just did not openly "date" in the way that dating is commonly understood in more western cultures. On the contrary, being openly seen together in public on a regular basis would be scandalous – something just not done. A couple in those circumstances might legally marry just to explicitly declare their exclusivity for each other in terms of their commitment to marriage, even if they are not ready to have the large time intensive cultural wedding celebration.

Another reason to keep the legal union separate is that, historically, sensitive financial issues could be discussed in more depth at the legal wedding. The sensitivity and intensely private nature of family matters involving finance could sometimes be better addressed in the context of a smaller private gathering between the families involved rather than in the ongoing dinner party atmosphere of the cultural wedding, where ears are open, drink flows freely and the taroffing never ends.

Practically, too, there's the matter of time. A bride or her family may not have her Jaheeziyeh ready yet, and the couple may want to have a legal wedding to formally cement the marriage now and wait to celebrate it with the community later.

The legal wedding can occur up to a year in advance of the formal and more public cultural wedding ceremony.

Iranians make a point of choosing a special day for luck. That perfect special day may be many months away. If no suitable date of good luck for the couple is available soon, why should the couple wait all that time? After all, they have a life together to build! Meaning, there's the chance factor. A joyous marriage can't take place if a beloved family member has passed away as the time of marriage approaches, which does happen. A decent interval of time must pass, so the marriage must be postponed.

The Persian wedding takes time, and while all involved will tell you it is time well spent, it can take place just as well whether the couple at its center are legally united or not. Should the couple be ready to unite before they are ready for the larger cultural wedding, then let them have their legal wedding.

RELIGIOUS CEREMONIES

What about religious ceremonies? Here I must defer to the particular tradition of the bride and groom. In the Persian wedding, it is customary to have religious references to the faith or faiths of the bride and groom; and religious guests (a Coptic priest, a rabbi, an Imam and so on) are as welcomed and honored as any other guests. But just as the Persian wedding is not a legal ceremony, it is also not a religious ceremony, and this is completely understood by all participants.

I don't feel qualified to give more than just general advice here. Those who want to place the seal of a formal religion on their union need to speak to an appropriate representative of that faith or those faiths. There are, after all, tens of thousands of established faiths and sects. Virtually all of them know certain members will marry persons of a different faith, and virtually all of them have ceremonies and practices that respectfully incorporate the spouse of another faith into a marriage to someone of their own faith. What those ceremonies and practices are, though, are unique to each faith, and every Persian spouse must address their questions to an appropriate representative of his or her faith.

The thing to always remember is that the Persian cultural wedding is there for the sake of the couple; the couple is not there for the sake of the wedding. If religious elements are wanted by the couple, they are added. If not, they are not.

And with these parts addressed, and kept in mind, we can now finally give our close attention to the events on the actual day of marriage in the (cultural) Persian wedding.

Chapter 21:
The Start of the Day

The Persian cultural wedding begins with the bride. At the start of the day, the bride (who has been resting the day before, in preparation for a long night of festivities) will be putting the last touches on her appearance at a salon with her bridal party. Or, the whole salon staff may be called on to appear at a (hopefully large) area of her home or at her hotel suite.

Once she's ready, the groom will come to the suite, knock on the door and get his first look at his bride. The groom always comes personally to pick her up and to bring her to the ceremony. He also, always, brings her a bouquet of flowers and a gift of jewelry. When she's ready to depart, he takes her to his car or a specially designated vehicle and off they go together.

Chapter 22:
The Burning of the Espand

Before the couple arrive and enter the space of the Sofreh Aghd to be married, the mothers and/or grandmothers of the bride and groom will burn espand for the couple before they sit.

The espand itself is simply a traditional collection of spices that are burned, much as incense is burned, and with much the same effect. But the burning of the espand is a formal ritual, and it is rich with symbolic meaning. The purpose of the burning the espand is to ward off "evil eyes" – that is, people who have negative, jealous or otherwise impure wishes for the couple. The espand is intended to neutralize any negative energy around the couple and protect them as they enter.

Tips: espand are burned by placing them on

coals, so be sure your coal is nice and hot. Also, be
sure you have beautiful and appropriately shaped
flowers available – the espand is traditionally placed
in the "cup" formed by the flower petals. Roses and
tulips hold espand wonderfully; daisies do not.

CHAPTER 23

THE PERSIAN WEDDING CEREMONY

STEP BY STEP

Preliminary Rites

BEFORE THE ARRIVAL OF THE COUPLE

The Aghd is the actual marriage ceremony. It is traditionally much smaller than the reception that follows. While there's no hard number to observe, normally only fifty people at the most and generally less, will be invited to the Aghd. By contrast, the reception to follow (the Jashn-Aroosi) can soar to 500 guests and more!

It should be noted that if this ceremony is held in a home, it's held in the home of the bride's family, even though all wedding and reception costs are paid for by the groom. Also, and hopefully needless to say, any preliminary necessities or rituals that need to be completed at this point are done. For instance, religious Muslims will often have a lamb sacrificed before the ceremony. The meat is then blessed, prepared and given to the poor.

Preparing for the Aghd

Traditionally, out of respect to the couple, the guests invited to the Aghd itself stand. Only the bride and groom should be seated at the Sofreh Aghd, though of course there should be a few seats available close to the Sofreh Aghd for the elderly or for those who can't stand. As modern traditions begin to take form, this is one aspect that is changing. At my own wedding, we had around 100 seats for guests; the rest were standing. Many couples are choosing to make the Aghd ceremony larger and larger in modern times. This I think is beautiful as the Aghd is such a beautiful and traditional ceremony where everyone is sure to enjoy themselves.

The Sofreh Aghd is set up in a room dedicated to the ceremonials. The candles on the Sofreh Aghd are lit just before the arrival of the couple. The coals for the espand are warmed, so espand may be burned as they enter.

Persian music begins. Any (traditional or otherwise appropriate) song will do, but lively Persian music is more commonly played as the couple enters.

As the Couple Arrives

As the bride and groom arrive, espand is burned for them. The music is playing, and it is always beautiful and often lively. My husband and I walked down the aisle to the "Persian Wedding Song," which begins like the traditional American wedding march and then breaks into a full-on Persian version. We had everyone dancing down the aisle as we approached the Sofreh Aghd, and it was so much fun!

Of course the pace and choice of music rests with the bride, the groom and their families. But expect enthusiasm, and lots of it, including cheering and traditional cries of *"le le le le le!"* -- the Persian hurrah!

Sitting at the Sofreh Aghd

The groom sits to the right of the bride. This is a sign of respect for him. As the couple sit, the music will fade, and the jubilant cheering and the *"le le le le le"* will eventually stop. (A Jewish friend of mine told me an interesting story about the possible origin of the *"le le le le le"* you'll hear in excitement and celebration during Middle Eastern festivities. She said this originates from the story in the Hebrew Scriptures of Jacob being tricked into marrying Leah. Women sought to warn Jacob, who thought he was marrying Rachel, that it was not Rachel but Leah, veiled, who approached him to be his bride. As they cried, "It's Leah. Leah! Leah!" the cries sounded like "Le-Le-Le-Le-Le!")

And when the music fades, and the cheering falls away, the ceremony begins.

The Ceremony

Since the Persian wedding ceremony is not a legal ceremony as such (except in Iran), anyone can officiate it. There are even couples who want to simplify the wedding process and have a legal official officiate over their union.

Whoever the person leading the ceremony for the couple may be, it is his (or her) responsibility to welcome the guests. If the ceremony is to be conducted in Farsi, this will be explained. A program will be provided for non-Farsi speaking guests, so they can follow along as well.

The person officiating will generally open the ceremony with a prayer from the religious book of the couple or with a poem from one of the many famous Persian poets.

As the ceremony begins, the mother of the bride or groom should take the Holy Book from the Sofreh Aghd and put it into the laps of the couple. It should be opened to a page with a text special to the couple.

Holding The Veil, Rubbing The Sugar Loaves

Also as the ceremony begins, the unmarried female family members of the bride and groom will take the veil from the Sofreh Aghd and hold it over the head of the bride and groom.

At the same time, happily married women in the family of the bride and groom will line up to "rub the sugar loafs" over the veil. The mother of the bride or groom should take the sugar loafs from the Sofreh Aghd and direct who comes to the Sofreh Aghd to rub the sugar loafs for the couple; but the general order is grandmothers and mothers of the bride and groom first; then elder married family members rub the sugar; then younger.

In the old days some women would purposely try to break a nice large piece of the sugar loaf off, which, if it happened, meant extra luck for the couple, for the purpose of rubbing the sugar loafs together over the heads of the bride and groom is to wish them sweetness in marriage and life. Once the veil is down, the sugar pieces are sometimes shaken off over the heads of the single girls, who welcome the extra luck as they hope for a good match.

Addressing The Couple

As the women line up and rub the sugar loafs for the couple, the leader of the ceremony is takes the couple through traditional ceremonial questions. He or she will begin with this phrase:

"[Name of Bride], daughter of [Bride's Father] and [Name of Groom], son of [Groom's Father], I am Vakhil [attorney/officiate of the couple], to marry the couple with the agreed upon Mariyeh [Dowry]"

Next the ceremonial leader will ask the bride, her eyes cast down throughout, the following:

"[Name of Bride], with the agreed upon Mariyeh [Dowry], do I have permission from you to perform this marriage?"

The bride will not respond. She lets her groom wait, to show she has thought this through. Instead the women in the bride's and groom's family say:

"No, she has gone to get the rosewater!"

Then the mother of the groom will come and

offer a piece of jewelry to the bride to convince her to accept and to marry the groom. (This is called "Zir Laf Zee.")

"Jewelry given to the bride, to honor her"

Next the ceremonial leader will also try to convince the bride to marry the groom, by reciting a beautiful poem about love, rosewater or marriage.

"A poem is read for the bride"

The poem is then read. At its conclusion, the ceremonial leader will ask the bride again:

"[Name of Bride], with the agreed upon Mariyeh [Dowry], do I have permission from you to perform this marriage?"

Again, the bride will not respond! She sits there silently and waits. But the women of the bride's family and the groom's will exclaim:

"She went to the garden to pick flowers!"

The mother of the groom will then approach the bride and offer her more jewelry or gold coins.
Then the ceremonial leader will again read her

a beautiful poem about love, marriage or flowers, to encourage the bride to accept.

"A poem is read for the bride."

Finally, for the third time the bride will be asked by the ceremonial leader:

"[Name of Bride], with the agreed upon Mariyeh [Dowry], do I have permission from you to perform this marriage?"

This time, the bride speaks, and says:

"Ba ejazeh Madar, va Pedar, va Bazorg tar-ha-Baleh!" (*"With the permission of my mother, father and the elders in my family - Yes!"*)

Once those present hear the word *"Baleh,"* yes, meaning the bride has accepted, the room explodes, erupting in ecstatic celebration and an avalanche of cries of *"le,le,le,le, le "* will soar.

At this point the groom will be asked the same phrase. No elaborate persuasion will be needed. The groom accepts the first time, and the veil held above their heads will gracefully come down .

Shabash

As the veil comes down, the couple is shabashed en masse by their family members. Shabash is the act of showering the couple with money, flowers or rice in celebration of their agreement to be married. Be sure your photographers are aware this extravagant shabash is coming, so they'll be appropriately positioned to capture the moment!

After the Couple Agrees to be Married

At this point if there are any legal or religious phrases which need to be read to formally legalize or legitimize the marriage, it is done here. Also, if the girl has chosen to remain veiled through the ceremony, at this point the groom offers her a piece of jewelry to honor her, and the veil is lifted by a female family member.

The groom gazes at his bride in the reflection of the mirror at the end of the Sofreh Aghd. He then turns to her and they then have their first kiss.

The Feeding of the Honey

The feeding of the honey symbolizes a sweet start to their married life. A sister or female family member of the couple will take the honey tray off the Sofreh Aghd and come offer it to the couple. The groom will be offered the honey first, so he may have the privilege of giving the honey to his bride first. The groom will take his right fifth (pinky) finger and dip it ever so lightly into the honey and offer it in this way to the bride. The bride will sometimes taste the honey and sometimes playfully bite the finger of the groom.

The bride is then offered the honey and feeds her groom in the same way.

Henna at the Aghd

If the couple did not choose to have a Hana-Bandan (see chapter 19), then this is the time when they complete the Hana-Bandan Ceremony. (Remember to have something with which the couple can wipe their hands after they're done.)

Exchange of Rings

At this point the couple will exchange rings. The rings are brought before the couple on a beautifully decorated tray by a female family member. The groom gives the bride her ring first. The bride then offers the groom his wedding band.

Signing of the Marriage Contract

Next, the couple may sign their formal marriage contract.

Giving of Gifts to the Couple

Now that the couple is married, it's time to present one's gifts. The couple is seated at the Sofreh Aghd, and the first gift-givers to approach them are their families. The mother and father of the groom come first.

The groom receives anything from watches, to money, to cufflinks. The bride always receives one thing: jewelry. Lots of jewelry. *Expensive* jewelry. The groom's family always makes sure they provide plenty of jewelry for the bride, and additional gifts of gold and jewelry are in such abundance that a female family member normally stands nearby with a beautifully decorated bag to contain it all.

On a planning note, there will be so many valuables present you will almost certainly want to have a security guard discretely present too, and there must be a secure locked location for the jewelry to be kept after the Aghd Ceremony. Especially for my non-Persian brides who have never witnessed this, remember: it's really quite amazing how *much* jewelry may be given, so be prepared to have a place to securely store it all!

Brides leave the ceremony as decorated in jewelry as a queen. Is it any secret, then, why Iranian brides should feel like queens on this most special of days.

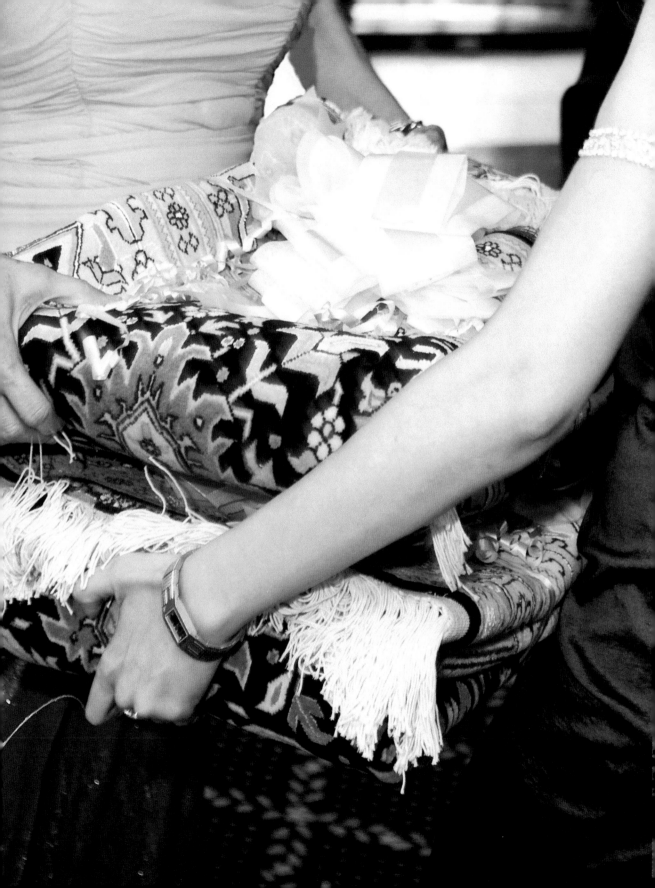

The Couple Departs

If the couple is moving to a new location for the reception, then they'll take a rose, turn it upside down and use it that way to burn out the flames from the candles on their Sofreh Aghd. If they wish to leave the Sofreh Aghd up during the reception, they can come back and burn the candles out at the end of the reception.

While any song may be played as the couple enters, the song Mobarak Baad – "Congratulations!" – is played for the couple as they depart.

And that's the end of the ceremony!

(But *not* of the partying!)

Chapter 24:
Releasing the Doves

(OR BUTTERFLIES)

It's customary to release either doves or butterflies into the open air after the ceremony has concluded. Who releases them? The couple release them together.

If you're buying caged birds or butterflies for the wedding, either buy them immediately before the ceremony (and be certain you call and reserve the purchase from the seller long in advance) or be sure you know how to care for and feed the butterflies and birds till their release. You don't want them to be too hungry and tired to fly off when the time comes – you want them to be as vibrant and full of life as the crowd and the couple!

CHAPTER 25

THE
RECEPTION!

Chapter 25:
Jashn-Aroosi

THE WEDDING RECEPTION

The Jashn-Aroosi is the wedding reception – the grand finale that wraps up the wedding day ceremonies in a massive, exciting, incredible party where everyone eats, drinks and dances themselves silly all night long and beyond. Seriously: the Jashn-Aroosi sometimes involves serving the guests breakfast when it's over.

Where is it held? The home of the groom – if there's enough room! The

Jashn-Aroosi can be small, including only a few dozen people; but it can also bring together as many as 500-1,000 people or even more. If the house of the groom just can't fit them in, a public venue is usually selected.

Who pays for it? The family of the groom pays

for it. They pay for the wedding and the reception is considered part of it.

THE RECEPTION

As I said, the reception is generally large. Virtually all the acquaintances of the couple or their families are invited, or, at the very least, welcome if they show up. Traditionally, in Iran, there was an open door at the groom's home where people could wander in freely to enjoy the wedding reception. When my father in-law was a young man in Kazerun, Iran, he told me they would leave for seven days at a time to travel to nearby towns, just to enjoy all the wedding festivities with an open door policy.

In part too, the reception is large because it is a presentation of the marriage to the entire community and a presentation that is intended to dazzle. The families want everyone to be impressed. How impressed can they be if they're not there? Of course, the whole community is invited! This applies as well to expatriate communities. There is probably no major city on earth without an Iranian community. When someone in that community marries, a good chunk if not all the community can be expected to attend the reception. Period. My fellow non-Iranians, remember this when you're forming a guest list. As a non-Iranian, I was a little shocked at how many guests from the local Persian community had to be invited. Not just them either, if maman-bazorg (grandma) & baba-bazorg (grandpa) of an invited guest were in town from Iran during the wedding, they were, obviously, implicitly invited too. You can see how the guest list can soar to over 500 without even trying very hard at all.

But large doesn't mean impersonal. Far from it! Get creative when it comes to your reception! Few events in the Persian wedding series of events are less scripted, and so you have full opportunity to be as colorful with decorations, wild with music or amazing with the cuisine as you like. Take your guests away for the evening into an enchanting and wildly fun experience like no other! Hookah bars, hot tea bars, traditional floor seating and sweets are placed all over for guests to enjoy until the sweets seem part of the décor – it all works, and it all works wonders when it comes to receiving fabulous comments on your Persian wedding and reception.

I speak from experience. In traditional Iranian weddings, for example, I learned that guests would be treated to hookahs (water pipes); so at my own wedding I made sure we had a seven-hookah bar outside on the patio of the country club where our wedding was hosted. We included a Persian hot tea bar where the hookahs were. Thinking only our Iranian guests would enjoy this hookah bar we were very wrong indeed! Everyone, especially the American guests, adored the tea and the hookahs! These things are not very expensive to do and they go a long way in creating a lasting impression at your own reception. Inside, we had both traditional floor seating and regular tables with chairs. Some went, with delight, straight for the floor- again, especially our American guests who found it so interesting and different, while some went straight for the chairs. We had Persian sweets scattered everywhere, from the entrance, to the ceremony room and throughout the reception hall for guests to enjoy all evening at their leisure, wherever they might happen to be. They loved it!

Remember that the reception is not only a chance for the whole community to celebrate the marriage. It's also an opportunity to unwind. All the important ceremonies and traditions which needed to be conformed to closely, have been at this point. Now it's time to enjoy and relax. So, at the reception, the idea is not to make sure that certain traditions are precisely observed. The idea is to eat drink and be merry. As a result, there really aren't too many traditional observances to follow at the reception, other than to show up, shabash the happy couple a few times and start dancing toward the cuisine.

But there are at least a few reception traditions you should still be aware of: the entrance of the bride and groom; the Persian Knife Dance; and the the Daste-be-Datse ritual that allows the bride's father to unite the couple for one final time, although the reception may well go on for several more hours.

THE ENTRANCE OF THE COUPLE

The bride and groom will be welcomed to the reception with lively up-beat Persian music and triumphant cheers from the guests to kick-off the night of celebration. The moment they arrive and every time they dance together they will be shabashed endlessly. They may have already been heavily shabashed at the earlier ceremonies. It doesn't matter. They'll be shabashed again throughout the reception, over and over. Whenever they dance together in the

evening they will also be shabashed! In fact, they will be shabashed so often throughout the reception that a family member should be delegated to collect all the shabash money for the couple and place it in a bag.

THE PERSIAN KNIFE DANCE

If you see the sister of the groom grab a knife and start dancing around the couple with it, and then a few more young women join in, don't jump to any colorful conclusions! This is a Persian tradition called the Knife Dance. What happens is that the sister of the groom (or bride) steals the knife from the cake-cutting table just before the couple is about to cut the cake. The sister dances around the couple with the knife and refuses to give it back until he pays her some token amount. As soon as he does, she passes off the knife to another young woman, and when she's paid off, the next young woman takes up the knife.

Sounds like a tough way to get to the cake, I know, but I can assure you that when it's done, everyone laughs and loves it. This is one of the classic fun traditions at Iranian receptions.

DASTE-BE-DATSE

A special moment occurs at the very end of the evening: a small tradition called Daste-be-Datse, meaning, "Hand-in-hand." In Daste-be-Datse, the father of the bride takes his daughter's hand and places it in the hand of the groom, giving her away for the last time.

When this happens, the ceremony ends, and the couple may leave the reception – although they will also be shabashed again one last time before they leave.

And if the candles of the Sofreh Aghd are still lit, the couple should now take a rose and burn the light out themselves.

THE END OF THE RECEPTION

Does this mean that the Persian wedding reception is over? Not at all. The wedding itself may be over and the bride and groom may have left, but the celebrations go on till late. Very very late. So late, in fact, that you should prepare to serve guests breakfast if it's going to be one of those marathon receptions all through the night and into the morning.

The good news is that you almost certainly won't have as many to serve as when you started. For it's a safe bet that dozens, if not hundreds, will have been wiped out in the grand manner and gone home already. But for a hardy surviving remnant, a parting breakfast is traditional.

(Tip: make the breakfast light. If they haven't managed to stuff themselves by now, something is wrong with their digestive systems!)

Notes On The Food at the Reception

There is so much food available at a Persian wedding that you are sure to find a place for your particular favorites. But overall, the kinds of foods tend toward the traditional Persian fare of kabob, rice and stews.

The choice of cuisine, of course, is up to the couple, except one dish that is always served-the wedding rice, Shrini Polo.

Shirin Polo

A Persian wedding is absolutely overflowing with food all the time. Surprisingly, though, there's only one food that is always served at a Persian Wedding: the wedding rice, called Shirin Polo.

Shirin is a Farsi word that means sweet and Polo means rice, so Shirin Polo means "Sweet Rice." Shirin Polo is a vegetarian rice dish made from Basmati Rice, mixed with the zest of an Orange, candied almonds, pistachios and spices.

It is very easy to make and relatively easy and inexpensive for a chef or caterer to acquire the ingredients.

Fruits and Nuts

Whenever you arrive at a Persian home, you will typically be offered fruits, nuts and tea. It's customary to offer these to guests no matter how long they're going to be there – five minutes or five hours.

It's the same way at Persian weddings, only more so.
People may have lavish fruit spreads that cover
entire tables and are beautifully decorated for the

guests to enjoy. It's more than a fruit buffet – it's an
art form. It certainly adds to the aesthetic beauty of
the celebration, and for Iranian guests the presence of
fruit will be a given.

Be sure to specifically request a wide variety
of fruits and to emphasize aesthetic beauty when
it comes to its presentation. Can the chef or caterer
create something beautiful that can cover an entire
table? Very probably. Ask!

Nuts are also commonly offered to guests by

Persian hosts. In fact, there's a world-famous Iranian nut store called "Tavazo" located in Tehran. When you walk into this store, the emphasis placed in Persian Culture on nuts will immediately be clear. Bins of nuts from all over the world cover the store from wall to wall. Iran is known for its pistachios in particular, so try to have some beautifully displayed pistachios in your nut display.

Yes, just as there must be a dazzling fruit display with a wide variety of fruits, there must be a dazzling nut display with a wide variety of nuts. You can keep costs reasonable, even so: it's entirely acceptable to mix expensive and inexpensive nuts. The criteria are variety and taste, not expense.

Pistachios are a given, however. You must have plenty of pistachios on hand even if they are a little expensive. But feel free to add another two or three nut varieties that are less expensive but displayed nicely. (Peanuts or heavily salted nuts? No.) Think walnuts or almonds, unprocessed, unsalted, pure and yummy.

When it comes to your display, be creative. Think outside of the box. Fruits and nuts don't nec-essarily have to be displayed in a bowl. Make sure you work out the display beforehand because you don't want the most impressive and tasty nuts sitting off to one side in a small nondescript bowl. If you *must* go with a bowl, definitely make it a fine glass or a crystal bowl. Find decor at your local decorat-ing store and decorate the bowl with gold flowers or pretty shiny ribbons that match your Sofreh's theme colors. Make it elaborate – there's no going over the top at a Persian wedding or reception. Be colorful, flashy, dare I say gaudy. In Persian weddings, bigger and creative showmanship is always better. Creativity is treasured, and creativity and open-mindedness are key traits to look for in your vendors. Look for excited vendors who are really up to it and let them go all the way in their plans and designs. Let them bounce all the ideas off you that they can.

TEA (CHAI)

The Farsi word for tea is chai. There should be cascades of Persian tea for guests to enjoy; they should overflow from large urns. Tea-drinking is very much a part of Persian culture: Iranians drink tea, piping hot, morning, noon, and night. Time and occasion make no difference. Everyone drinks tea all day long, and tea is offered to all guests in a Persian home and certainly at a Persian wedding.

Any particular brand? Teas from Iran itself make a nice touch, but any high-quality tea, from Earl Grey to Darjeeling, are welcome. I would specify hot tea to your chef or caterer. Again, display matters. Ask your vendor if he or she can display the cups and saucers in nicely arranged stacks or on suitable display. The more aesthetic beauty at your reception, the more it will be appreciated and commented upon. It costs nothing but a little time or effort to stack tea saucers beautifully, but it is one more addition to a wealth of overall beauty and the effect will not fail to impress.

PERSIAN BEEF KABOB (KABOB KUBIDEH)

Persian Beef Kabob is the quintessential Persian food. When I met my husband, I told him once I

wanted some comfort food. He asked me, "What's comfort food?" Though he was born and raised in the United States, he was raised by Iranian parents in an Iranian household, and American catch phrases were not part of his upbringing. To this very day, I could speak to my husband in American catch phrases and he would have no idea what I am saying. I find this fascinating given that he grew up all his life in the United States! After I explained the concept of comfort food to him, he exclaimed in excitement, "Oh I get it! You want Kabob!" I could not stop laughing. It was so funny.

It was funny, but serious too. For some beef kabob is just beef kabob. For Persians, beef kabob is a Persian tradition and they take Persian tradition seriously! So you most definitely do not want microwave beef kabobs from the supermarket at your reception.

Traditional fare must be made traditionally and lovingly. It must be made of either beef or lamb, with finely minced onions and spices. It must not be diced up into chunks of meat, like shish kabobs. Each one must be a single piece of meat, properly flattened and then grilled on a long, flat metal skewer over an open flame.

CHICKEN KABOB (JUJEH KABOB)

Jujeh is Farsi for "chicken." Beef kabob may be king, but the chicken kabob is another classic and perennial favorite of Persian cuisine.

This dish is all about the marinade that it must sit in before being grilled. The chicken pieces are marinated in lemon juice, saffron, minced onions and olive oil, for a good long time, before being grilled to perfection. It is a simple recipe with a delicious result.

GARNISH FOR KABOBS

No Persian meal is complete without beautiful garnishes to top off the presentation and bring out the flavours of the meat. Tomatoes are commonly grilled with the meat dishes and served along with the meat dish. Sabzi, Soumak, turnips, lemon and lime are served to complement the meal.

Sabzi is Farsi for herbs. Sabzi is also a mixture of several herbs including parsley, mint, green onions and so on. It isn't generally dashed over the meal beforehand: normally it's displayed around the meat to be added, dabbed and enjoyed by the guest as desired. Soumak is a spice that can be ordered from any middle eastern store and usually is sprinkled over the kabob, giving it an even more delicious flavor.

MAST-EH KHEAR

Mast is the Farsi word for yogurt – *real* yogurt, not the artificially flavored kind sweetened with Splenda that you see at the supermarket. Khear (pronounced "Key-are") is the farsi word for cucumber; careful with the pronunciation my fellow non-Iranians. I once mis-spoke when I offered Mast-eh *Kir*, which led to an eruption of laughter in the room from my best friend Meitra and her sister Mahtab. "We don't want Kir!" Mast-eh *khear* (not Kir) is a cucumber yogurt dish that is so delicious you won't believe it. Often what puts it over the top is a generous hint of fresh mint and spices. I include Mast-eh khear in this section because it is commonly eaten with the Persian kabob and rice. If you have kabob and rice on your menu, put Mast-eh khear there also. To Iranians, it's like what a hot dog and a Coke are to Americans. You just don't have the one without the other.

PLAIN BASMATI RICE GARNISHED WITH SAFFRON

This dish is the base for the beef and chicken kabob dishes. The garnish for the rice is more rice which is stained a vibrant orange color by saffron. Did you know that, ounce for ounce, saffron is more expensive than gold? Fortunately you don't need an ounce to make this beautiful garnish transform the rice into a truly spectacular reception treat.

Part Five:

POST-WEDDING CELEBRATIONS

Chapter 26:
Patakhti and Madar Zan Salam

There's an American saying: "It ain't over till it's over." As far as Persian wedding protocol goes, even when it's over, it's not over! This isn't a bad thing – good food, good company and continuing celebrations never are. Less formal dinner and other get-togethers between family and friends continue post-wedding.

But there are three formal events which still need to take place to do everything just right: Madar Zan Salaam, Patakhti, and Pagosha.

The first two somewhat overlap. After the wedding, the groom goes to thank the mother of the bride for raising such a wonderful daughter. This is called Madar Zan Salaam, which is roughly translated as "saying hello to the mother." Also, a small party is thrown in the evening a few days after the wedding for the couple and their family to celebrate and remember the happy wedding. This is called Patakhti.

Madar Zan Salaam begins the morning of the day after the wedding; Patakhti takes place on the evening of third day after the wedding. Since those days, like all days connected with a Persian wedding, are worth celebrating, naturally they involve another opportunity to throw a party. These are more subdued parties, however: the crowds and the sprawling, ecstatic festivities of the Aghd are done and many a participant may be a little fatigued. Rarely is any participant in a Persian wedding so fatigued that they would turn down a chance to attend another such party, however, particularly when given in such a more soothing key

That's the keynote of the Madar Zan Salaam and the Patakhti: not wild revelry, but rather a sense of calm congratulatory celebration between everyone involved, each knowing that a formal seal has been placed on something good and loving and that a new family has set sail with all possible blessings into the future.

Madar Zan Salaam

Madar Zan Salaam is the first of these two occasions to take place and one of the very few where dancing is not likely to occur. (Not very likely to occur, anyway.) The Madar Zan Salaam is as traditional as it is simple. On the morning after the wedding, the groom calls the mother of the bride to say hello, see that everything is well, say "Thank you" for all of her efforts and kindnesses and arrange to have lunch the day after next.

What follows is a lunch meeting between the mother of the bride, the bride and groom (with, optionally, a few close family members of the bride in tow). At this get-together the new husband must present himself properly as such to his new mother-in-law (and possibly one or two selected in-laws as well).

His manner is formal. The groom brings a basket of flowers or a box of sweets or a gold coin and offers it to his new mother-in-law. She will thank him for his thoughtfulness and ask that lunch be served. Over lunch, the groom will thank the mother-in-law for raising such a wonderful and beautiful wife, who (he assures her) he will certainly cherish and treasure forever.

The mother may then offer a gift to her daughter also, most likely a home furnishing of some sort, especially if the couple finds themselves unexpectedly short of a few pieces in the Jaheeziyeh[1]. With the couple's home properly finished, the newly married couple's life as householders may properly begin. Good conversation follows as the mother-in-law gets to know her son-in-law even better during this meeting.

This polite and almost serene new approach is a definite variation on the old-fashioned way of concluding the Madar Zan Salaam. Classically, the groom is expected to steal some item from the home of the bride; indeed, a groom inclined towards traditionalism will keep an eye peeled for some particularly choice item to filch from the home of the bride as early as the Hana-Bandan or even as early as the Namzadi.

This is not done to honor kleptomania, but rather metaphor: taking the item playfully symbolizes that he has stolen the daughter. Taking it may not be particularly easy to do, though: women on the bride's side of the family are in on the game, so they make a point to keep a close eye on the groom to make sure he doesn't steal a thing! Of course they want him to succeed, and some may even look in the other direction if a suitable groom lacks the flair

[1]Please refer to chapter 17 on the Jaheeziyeh.

CHRISTEN FLACK BEHZADI, M. D.

for larceny. (The groom may not always work alone, either: a female family member of the groom may do the theft during one of the negotiations when all the attention is on the groom.)

Usually, however, the feeling is that the groom should earn his theft all on his own, through honest dishonest effort, just as he should earn his bride. No strain, no gain.

Once the groom succeeds, he cheerfully and ecstatically announces the theft to the family, saying, "I have stolen your daughter!" At which point everyone laughs and applauds and congratulates him for getting away with it.

But he doesn't get to keep whatever he's taken. During Madar Zan Salaam, the groom returns the item he has taken to his new mother-in-law, along with presents such as flowers, sweets or a gold coin.

The symbolism is plain: a daughter that has been taken is now returned. And a new son is given.

The Madar Zan Salaam then fades into the background, until that third evening making way for what comes immediately next: the Patakhti.

PATAKHTI

The Patakhti takes place later in the evening on the third day after or very soon after the wedding.

The family of the bride sends sweets from their home to the new home of the newly married couple. The sweet is called Kachie (Caaa-Qi), and it is a heavy sweet intended to give the bride extra energy.

Originally the Patakhti was a ladies-only affair, but now those throwing the party may host it the traditional way or invite whomever they choose. The Patakhti is normally hosted at the largest home of either family, but this is not set in stone.

As you might expect, there is food, there is dancing, sweets and fruits are plentiful, hot tea is flowing and gifts continue to be showered on the newly married couple: crystal, gold coins, money, etc.

In fact, in many parts of Iran no gifts are given during the Jashn-Aroosi and this is the when the gifts are given. The bride dresses exquisitely – she knows she is both the center of attention and is also being subtly assessed in her new role as wife; so she remains on her best behavior.

In terms of tone, the Patakhti has something of the feel of a successful post-game analysis in sports. The wedding has been accomplished. It has been pulled off – magnificently, to be sure. Talk invariably centers on how things went, the loveliness of the bride, the good looks of the groom, the incredible food and so on and so on.

The Patakhti allows everyone involved to recollect with a certain tranquility all the labor and efforts involved in putting together a truly unforgettable event, and also to savor again the joy and highlights

of that event and seal it in memory.

Like soft music after a symphonic climax, the Patakhi allows the families and participants to recall the pleasures of what they have experienced and to look forward to what is to come for the happy new couple and for the newly linked families.

Everyone has a very good time.

Chapter 27:
PaGosha

A NEVER-ENDING ENDING

PAGOSHA

PaGosha is one of the more intimate steps of the Persian wedding process. No small part of its charm rests with the fact that it takes place after the wedding and may continue to take place several times more.

What exactly is PaGosha? It might best be described as being asked over for a wonderful family dinner with your new family – again and again and again.

PaGosha begins with an invitation to dinner from the family of the bride. Normally the invitation is not given till at least a week or two after the wedding ceremony, so the couple can enjoy their honeymoon, return, and take the time to rest and recuperate from the many preceding events.

The invitation is commonly sent during Madar Zan Salaam – not the award-winning Iranian movie by that name directed by Khosro Malekan, but directly after the wedding. The invitation is extended by the "elders" of the family first. If tradition is followed strictly, the elders who send along the invitation are the great-grandparents or grandparents of the bride. But a sufficiently senior aunt or uncle, or the oldest member of the family, whatever the exact relation, may be called upon to send it as well. Though family elders are the ones to send the invitation, it is always the mother of the bride who is the first host.

What is the symbolic mystical significance of the PaGosha? What ancient ritualistic meaning drives the gathering of these people to dinner? The meaning that brings them together is – just to have dinner! To welcome the groom and bride into each other's families, warmly, comfortably and happily.

While the extended and extensive process of negotiations and discussions and meetings and parties that make up the preliminaries to the wedding definitely serves to acquaint members of each family with one another, the fact remains that there is a certain underlying seriousness and formality to the entire process. Complex matters from finance to detailed discussions of event planning are involved. It can be spectacular and it can be fun, but it is always rich with the quiet welcoming glow of a family gathering. PaGosha serves to cultivate exactly that kind of quiet, deep sense of peace and understanding: to deepen the awareness that home and family are now here and are now one.

You may ask, "Isn't all that a heavy burden for one single dinner to carry? You can hardly expect that kind of family feeling to develop over just one meal." Quite right – that's why the PaGosha isn't just one dinner, but a whole string of dinners. The elders invite the new couple over one night; and then the bride's sisters one after the other invite them over for dinner; and then the bride's brothers invite the couple over; and then the bride's aunts, and uncles, and cousins, and extended family, until, well, everyone on the bride's side of things invites the couple over.

And then? Then everyone on the groom's side of the family, one after the other after the other, invites the couple over. Even unrelated friends of the groom invite them over to dinner, just as the unrelated friends of the bride do too, all so the bride can get to know and be comfortable with the friends of the groom and vice versa.

Are there rules to the PaGosha or is it as casual and free-form as it appears? It's as casual and as free-form as it appears. Of course, the hosts try to cook

the favorite foods of the bride and groom; the bride and groom generally offer a basket of flowers to the hosts; and the hosts generally give gifts to the bride and groom. But then that generally happens anyway.

And when is the PaGosha over? It might be said to be formally concluded when everyone on both sides of the family have had the couple over for dinner once. At that point, the couple begins to reciprocate by inviting family and friends over to their new home for dinner. Which is then followed by the family and friends inviting the couple over to their place again; which is followed by the couple inviting them over again; which is followed by...

Or to put it another way: when is the PaGosha really over? Never.

Endless Love

STAY IN TOUCH AT
WWW.WeddingPersian.COM

I want to sincerely thank all of you for joining me on this fantastic journey. My wish is that you have every tool you need to host your very own Persian Wedding. I hope you're ecstatic and thrilled for your upcoming Persian Wedding now that you know how to throw such a truly great, truly Persian event!

Please feel free to let others know about this book or to share your thoughts and ideas about it on Twitter or Facebook or in an Amazon review. I'd love to hear from you! And if you're ever unsure of what to do or if you need more information or inspiration, please don't hesitate to leave a message for me at the Persian Wedding Book website at www.weddingpersian.com, or to email me at christen@weddingpersian.com.

Ceremonies end, but love is forever. I wish you happy wedding planning, a happy wedding, and an even happier married life!

Love,
Christen

About The Author

Christen Flack Behzadi was born in Oklahoma City and raised in West Bloomfield, Michigan. A life-long lover of cultures and celebrations of all kinds, Christen met her soulmate Pedram "Bubby" Behzadi in medical school at the University of Oklahoma in 2005. Meeting Pedram's family and friends made her more and more familiar with the richness and depth of Persian culture, which led to her determination to have and her own beloved Persian Wedding. The attention to tradition, the supreme beauty and symbolism, and the divine love evident throughout wedding celebrations led Christen to believe that everyone should experience, have, enjoy and understand the Persian Wedding – whether they're Persian or not! So while continuing to finish her medical residency, she worked for almost four years researching and writing this descriptive guide to help other brides, grooms and families both Persian and new to Persian culture to better plan and understand their own Persian Wedding celebrations.

Dr. Christen Flack Behzadi, M.D., currently practices Anesthesiology, and lives with her husband, who practices Emergency Medicine, in upstate New York. She spends her free time working on future books, including her first novel, and *Simple Persian Cooking (Even If You Have No Idea What Persian Means)*.

ACKNOWLEDGMENTS
AND
REFERENCES

ACKNOWLEDGMENTS

I would like to sincerely thank everyone who helped me to see the creation of this book from an idea to the finished work.

First, I would like to thank Ms. Sara Karimi from Iranibooks. com who helped me locate copies of authentic and detailed out-of-print books on Persian Wedding customs. These books were the core and foundation of my research for this book, and I sincerely appreciate her working so hard to find those books for me.

My wedding planner Kim Cooper of Queen of Events is truly a creative genius. Kim, you epitomize what every bride would want from a planner: equal parts friend and creative genius, a calming presence in times of stress, and an organizing force when chaos threatened. Thank you for researching Persian culture and customs and making this a wedding beyond my dreams.

Similarly I want to thank my incredible Persian DJ Pedram "DJ Sultan" Farazandeh (djsultanpmi@yahoo.com) for creating such electrifying energy at the wedding and for serving as such an invaluable key vendor.

I thank my entire family and my sisters Courtney, Cathryn, Catelyn, Carey and Parisa for being such good sports and making the event so much fun. (Every bride has a story of a mini-disaster on her wedding day, and I want especially to thank my sister Cathryn for helping me keep my sanity after a slight wardrobe malfunction left me staring at a beautiful but damaged wedding dress. Thank you for telling me I looked amazing, even though I had to wear my party dress to the ceremony.)

I would like to thank my mother, Jennifer for assisting as legal counsel and helping me with the endless agreements, contracts, negotiations, copyright assignments and paperwork for the editors, photographers, designers, and artists on the business side of this work. Without your help, I would probably be broke right now from legal fees!

Daddy, I thank you for giving me my dream wedding and for not saying no to me. If it were not for that event, this book would never be possible. Thank you for letting me just go for it.

When I began writing this book the only people in the world who knew were my mother-in-law, who was translating books on the subject for me, and my husband who was always whispering in my ear "You can do it!" I cannot describe how important that support, belief and blind faith from my dear Bubby Joon (Pedram) was for me. Somehow I began to believe him and kept writing despite every reason to believe I couldn't do this. Thank you for carrying me through to see my dream. Thank you for the blind faith.

Abu, thank you for introducing me to Persian culture,and for cooking us feasts while we would discuss chapters in the book and I would get translations from Mamani. Thank you for being my cultural consultant, and explaining the love and meaning behind the events. Thank you for telling me the stories about how you would leave school when you were a kid for a week when there was a wedding back home in Iran. Thank you for describing the richness of the events, and leaving that — and so much more — in my heart.

After the first manuscript was finally done I showed no one for two months. I was the only one who had ever laid eyes on the actual manuscript. The first person I gave a copy to look at and review was my sister Courtney Salesman, who is herself an extremely talented writer. I want to thank you Courtney for looking over the book, and for your positive feedback. You gave me so much confidence because I knew you would be honest and had the background to honestly evaluate the work.

Thank to all the photographers who contributed to the book, including John Retallack, Amanda Lassiter, and Chris Humphreys.

Thanks too to all my editors:

I want to thank my Grandmother, Virginia, a retired college English Professor for bringing back out the old red pen to help clean up the first version of the manuscript.

I would like to thank Jennifer Burrows of JSB Writing for your superb and very fast editing of the third round of the manuscript.

Thanks to my sister-in-law Parisa Behzadi: Parisa, your edits of the manuscript were priceless, because you helped me to understand beyond the grammatical issues to the cultural edits needed as well. Thank you for taking time from your trip to Iran edit the manuscript..

To my editor and friend David Pascal, I cannot ever thank you enough for all you have done for me to see this book come alive. Your encouragement, knowledge of the process and advice have been dearly appreciated.

And finally, my sincere gratitude to my mother-in-law, Roya; *Mamani*, when I think of your efforts, I have no words to adequately describe the love and devotion and dedication you showed for a solid year in preparing the sofreh aghd perfectly. Not only was your help with the book everything I could have asked, you were crucial in making the original event so wonderful that it inspired me in the first place.

Thank you, Mamani, for making that dream real. You are more than a mother-in-law to me and all of your behind-the-scenes work, from planning our wedding to helping me with this book, has been instrumental in making it come alive. All of your advice, love, assistance and devotion is sincerely appreciated. I am so grateful that of all the mother-in-laws in the world, God blessed me with you. You are the kindest soul, and I am grateful every day that you are in my life.

Thank you for all you've done. Thank you for your patience. Thank you for the best husband a girl could ever ask for.

REFERENCES

On line References

Zoroastrian Heritage Institute Online
http://www.heritageinstitute.com/zoroastrianism/

Iran Chamber Society Online
http://www.iranchamber.com/

Wikipedia:

Frankincense
http://en.wikipedia.org/wiki/Frankincense

Angelica
http://en.wikipedia.org/wiki/Angelica

Persian Marriage
http://en.wikpedia.org/wiki/Persian_wedding

http://en.wikipedia.org/wiki/Zoroastrian_wedding

Book References

Adams, Charles J., editor, Iranian civilization and culture : essays in honour of the 2,500th anniversary of the founding of the Persian Empire (1971: Toronto).

Iqbal, Afzal; foreword by Arberry, A. J. Life and work of Muhammad Jalal-ud-Din Rumi (1974)

Jadīd Al-Islām: The Jewish "New Muslims" of Meshhed. By Raphael Patai . 1997, Wayne State University Press

Boyce, Mary, Textual sources for the study of Zoroastrianism, Manchester: Manchester University Press (1984).

Boyce, Mary, "Ahura Mazdā", Encyclopaedia Iranica, 1 (1983).

Boyce, Mary, The History of Zoroastrianism, 1 (1975, repr. 1996).

Boyce, Mary, The History of Zoroastrianism, 2, (1982, repr. 1997).

Curtis, Vesta Sarkhosh, and Canby, Sheila R. Persian love poetry (2006)

Drunken universe : an anthology of Persian Sufi poetry (1987).

Duchesne-Guillemin, Jacques, "Zoroastrianism", Encyclopedia Americana, 29 (1988).

Farhangi, Reyhaneh, Jahaz Boran & Hana Bandan. Kelk-e-Azadegan Tehran, Iran. Kelkezadegan.com Published by Kelke Zadegan

Farhangi, Reyhaneh, Baleh Boran and Namzadi. Kelk-e-Azadegan Tehran, Iran. Kelk, ezadegan.com Published by Kelke Zadegan

Farhangi, Reyhaneh, Mahe Asal & Pagosha. Kelk-e-Azadegan Tehran, Iran. Kelkezadegan.com Published by Kelke Zadegan

Farhangi, Reyhaneh, Patakhti & Madar Zan Salaam. Kelk-e-Azadegan Tehran, Iran. Kelkezadegan.com Published by Kelke Zadegan

Farhangi, Reyhaneh, Ashnayi & Khastegari. Kelk-e-Azadegan Tehran, Iran. Kelkezadegan.com Published by Kelke Zadegan

Farhangi, Reyhaneh, Aghd & Aroosi. Kelk-e-Azadegan Tehran, Iran. Published by Kelke Zadegan , Kelkezadegan.com

Fitzgerald, Edward; Robinson, B. W., notes. Rubâiyât of Omar Khayyâm. (1979)

Foltz, Richard, Spirituality in the Land of the Noble: How Iran Shaped the World's Religions, (2004).

Mackey, Sandra; Harrop, W. Scott Harrop, research assistant; Iranians : Persia, Islam, and the soul of a nation (1996).

Malandra, William W., An Introduction to Ancient Iranian Religion. Readings from the Avesta and Achaemenid Inscriptions (1983).

Meisami, Julie Scott, Structure and meaning in Medieval Arabic and Persian Poetry: Orient Pearls (2003).

Miller, Margaret Christina, Athens and Persia in the fifth century B.C. : a study in cultural receptivity (1997).

Miller, Lloyd Clifton, Music and song in Persia : the art of Āvāz (1999).

Nasr, Seyyed Hossein; Razavi, Mehdi Amin, editor. Islamic intellectual tradition in Persia (1996).

Moridani, Bijan, The Persian Wedding, Copyright 2005 by Bijan Moridani. Published by Inner Layers.

Moulton, James Hope, The Treasure of the Magi: A Study of Modern Zoroastrianism (1917, repr. 1997).

Jalāl al-Dīn Rūmī, Maulana (Rumi). Fountain of fire : a celebration of life and love (1994)

Jalāl al-Dīn Rūmī, Maulana (Rumi); Barks, Coleman, Moyne John, Arberry, A.J., and Nicholson, Reynold, translators. Essential Rumi (1996)

Schimmel, Annemarie. Two-colored brocade : the imagery of Persian poetry

Settegast, Mary, When Zarathustra spoke : the reformation of neolithic culture and religion (2005).

Stolze, Franz, Die Achaemenidischen und Sasanidischen Denkmäler und Inschriften von Persepolis (1882).

Ali, Syed Ameer, Persian culture (1913).

Stern, Ephraim, Material culture of the land of the Bible in the Persian Period, 538-332 B.C. (1982).

Wilson, Peter Lamborn, and Pourjavady, Nasrollah, translations and commentary.

Jaffery, Yunus, editor, History of Persian literature (1981).

Made in the USA
Lexington, KY
27 December 2013